The Sacred Heart of Jesus

BY

SAINT JOHN EUDES

Translated by

DOM. RICHARD FLOWER, O.S.B., M.A.
OF THE PORTSMOUTH PRIORY
PORTSMOUTH, R. I.

With an Introduction by

THE REVEREND GERALD B. PHELAN
PRESIDENT OF THE PONTIFICAL INSTITUTE OF MEDIAEVAL STUDIES
TORONTO, CANADA

Loreto Publications
A.D. 2011

Imprimi Potest:
ALBERT D'AMOURS, C.J.M.
Praepositus Provincialis

Laval-des-Rapides, P.Q.,
die 14a decembris 1944

Nihil Obstat:
ARTHUR J. SCANLAN, S.T.D.
Censor Librorum

Imprimatur:
FRANCIS J, SPELLMAN, D.D.
Archbishop, New York

September 26, 1945

Published in 1946 by
P. J. Kenedy & Sons, New York

Published by

Loreto Publications
P. O. Box 603
Fitzwilliam, NH 03447
603.239.6671
www.loretopubs.org

ISBN 1-930278-35-7

Printed and Bound in the United States

GENERAL PREFACE

St. John Eudes has been called "the wonder of his age." Orator, founder, reformer of the clergy, he crowded into a life of seventy-nine years so many and such varied accomplishments that one marvels how a single man could achieve so much. In addition to the activities of an incessant and many-sided apostolate, he wrote a number of valuable books, which rank him as one of the most prolific ascetic writers of the seventeenth century.

For many years the devotional writings of St. John Eudes were practically unknown. Occasionally a volume was discovered in the library of some seminary or religious house. Many others preserved in manuscript form were lost in the chaos of the French Revolution. At the beginning of the present century the sons of St. John Eudes united in a tribute of filial piety to bring out a complete edition of the works of their spiritual father, seeking for them in public and private libraries throughout the world. About twenty volumes were found and edited in 1905 by the late Fathers Charles Lebrun, C.J.M., and Joseph Dauphin, C.J.M. This first edition in French, *Oeuvres Complètes du Vénérable Jean Eudes,* ran into twelve octavo volumes with introductions, explanatory notes, analytic and alphabetic indexes of great value. These writings constitute a complete summa of ascetic and pastoral theology. The list is as follows:

Volume I. The Life and the Kingdom of Jesus in Christian Souls. In this work the Saint develops his spiritual teaching on the Christian life, namely, that the Christian life is simply the life of Jesus extended and continued in each one of us.

Volume II. This volume contains six short treatises on subjects relating to the Christian life:

1. *A Treatise on the Respect Due to Holy Places,* which is an echo of the fiery denunciations he pronounced during his missions against profaners of the temple of God.

2. *Meditations on Humility,* a series of meditations on the profession of humility as used daily in his order of priests, the Congregation of Jesus and Mary.

3. *Interior Colloquies of the Soul with God,* meditations on creation, the end of man and the grace of Baptism.

4. *Man's Contract with God in Baptism,* a summary of the teachings of Sacred Scripture and Tradition on the Sacrament of Baptism.

5. *The Practice of Piety*, a brief explanation of what is necessary in order to live a Christian life.

6. *Catechism of the Mission*, an outline of the catechetical instructions given during the mission.

Volume III. It contains two important works on sacerdotal perfection:

1. *The Memorial of the Ecclesiastical Life*, an explanation of the dignity and duties of the priesthood.

2. *A Manual of Piety for use in an Ecclesiastical Community*, in which the author explains how the means of sanctification he recommended to his priests should be practically applied in their daily lives.

Volume IV. It comprises significant works on the priestly ministry.

1. *The Apostolic Preacher* is one of the first treatises written on the ministry of the Word of God and is even yet one of the most practical.

2. *The Good Confessor* explains the qualities and obligations of the minister of the Sacrament of Penance.

3. *Counsels for Mission Confessors* suggests practical means of assisting penitents to make their examination of conscience and excite themselves to contrition.

4. *The Manner of Serving Mass* explains the dignity and holiness of this service and what one must do to perform it devoutly and worthily.

Volume V. The Admirable Childhood of the Most Holy Mother of God. This book treats of the holy childhood of Mary and the practical means of honoring the mysteries and virtues of her early life.

Volumes VI, VII, VIII contain the entire writings of the Saint on the Sacred Hearts of Jesus and Mary. This work is entitled: *The Admirable Heart of the Mother of God.* It comprises twelve books covering the complete theology of the devotion to the Sacred Hearts. Eleven books discuss the theory, history and practice of the devotion to the Immaculate Heart of Mary. The last book deals with the devotion to the Sacred Heart of Jesus. It is this work, together with the Offices of the Sacred Hearts, that merits for him the title of Father, Doctor and Apostle of the Devotion to the Sacred Hearts.

Volume IX. The Rules and Constitutions of the Congregation of Jesus and Mary.

Volume X contains *The Rules and Constitutions of the Order of Our Lady of Charity*, the *Directory* of the Order, and a collection of two hundred and forty letters.

Volumes XI and *XII* embrace the Saint's *Liturgical Works*, comprising twenty-five Offices and Masses for feasts to which he urged special devotion, the *Memorial of God's Blessings* and several minor works.

The second French edition appeared in 1935, *Oeuvres Choisies de Saint Jean Eudes*, prepared under the direction of Father Lebrun, the leading authority on Eudistic research. It comprises nine volumes: *The Life and the Kingdom of Jesus, Meditations on Various Subjects, Regulae Vitae Christianae et Sacerdotalis, Man's Contract with God in Baptism, Letters and Minor Works, Writings on the Priesthood, The Sacred Heart of Jesus, The Admirable Heart of Mary*, and *The Admirable Childhood of the Mother of God*. The format of these volumes is compact and more convenient than the 1905 edition, which is now out of print.

The publication of the works of St. John Eudes revealed the extent and depth of their spiritual doctrine. Cardinal Pitra, who directed the Process of Beatification of the Saint in 1909, discovered in his writings a remarkable depth of thought and purity of doctrine. Cardinal Vives has more recently expressed his admiration:

I was acquainted with the Doctors of the Order of St. Francis; I was acquainted with Saint Teresa and Saint John of the Cross, the mystical writers of my own country, Spain; but I was completely ignorant of the writings of Father Eudes. As a member of the Sacred Congregation of Rites it was my duty to study his life and his works, and I am in admiration. Blessed John Eudes must be ranked with the great lights of the Church. His spiritual doctrine is profound and of wonderful exactitude. He is one of the writers who best expounded the doctrine of the Gospel.[1]

The late Father Ange Le Doré, for fifty years Superior General of the Congregation of Jesus and Mary, wrote:

The works of Blessed John Eudes, although they do not bear the scientific touch of the professional theologian, are nevertheless proof of his remarkable theological, ascetic and scriptural knowledge. . . . He is not a Doctor after the fashion of the scholastics of the thirteenth century or of the great theologians of the sixteenth and seventeenth centuries. As they, he might have built up theses and composed books didactic in form; but he was before all a saver of souls. For him the science of theology found its chief field of usefulness in the practice of virtue and in the acquisition of sanctity of which it is the principle. . . . He was a Doctor after the manner of the Apostles, the Fathers of the Church, St. Francis de Sales and St. Alphonsus de Liguori. The science which shines in his works not only emits light; it engenders piety and sanctity.[2]

[1] Quoted by Bray, *Saint John Eudes* (Halifax, 1925), p. 116.   [2] *Ibid.*, p. 117.

The doctrine expounded by St. John Eudes follows the school of Cardinal Pierre de Bérulle and Father Charles de Condren, prominent seventeenth-century ascetic writers. He applies this doctrine to the devotion to the Sacred Hearts of Jesus and Mary, developing and rendering it more precise and practical. He has the rare gift of expressing the most sublime truths in simple, familiar language. He also excels in condensing into a few pages a complete scheme of Christian life and perfection.

The wish was repeatedly expressed that these inspirational writings could be made available to English-speaking readers. Excellent abridged editions of certain books were published in England and in Canada, but they did not do justice to the literary value of the Saint. Consequently, the Eudist Fathers commemorating their tercentenary in 1943 resolved to publish a complete translation of the principal works of their founder. Competent translators were secured and much time and effort were expended to produce readable volumes in modern English, faithful to the spirit and style of the original.

The first English edition, *Selected Works of Saint John Eudes,* is the result. In presenting it to the public the Eudist Fathers and the Religious of Our Lady of Charity of the Refuge, and of the Good Shepherd, wish to thank all those who contributed to the success of this comprehensive undertaking. They are especially grateful to the distinguished churchmen who have so graciously accepted to introduce these volumes to Catholic readers, because they consider that the works of St. John Eudes should be more widely known. The Saint in his apostolic work and in his writings ranks with the eminent figures who belong not to one country and to one religious order but to the universal Church. Three centuries have passed since he wrote the works now being printed in the new world, a striking illustration of the truth that he wrote for all time. He still speaks in accents that penetrate the mind and heart of the reader to enlighten, purify and sanctify so that Jesus Christ may live and reign in the Christian soul.

WILFRID E. MYATT, C.J.M.
PATRICK J. SKINNER, C.J.M.
Editors

Holy Heart Seminary
Halifax, N. S.
Feast of St. John Eudes, 1945

CONTENTS

ix

MEDITATIONS

for

THE FEAST OF THE SACRED HEART OF JESUS

OTHER MEDITATIONS

on

THE SACRED HEART OF JESUS

MASS AND OFFICE
of
THE SACRED HEART OF JESUS

PRAYERS
to
THE SACRED HEART OF JESUS

INTRODUCTION

DEVOTION to the Sacred Heart of Jesus today ranks among the most appealing devotions in the liturgy. Its widespread popularity among the faithful, as well as the transcendent dignity of its object, gives to this devotion a place of high honor among the numerous devotions which the Spirit of God has raised up and fostered in the bosom of Holy Mother Church. Yet, it is a devotion of comparatively recent origin. Not until late in the seventeenth century did the Devotion to the Sacred Heart become firmly established in the Church. At that period God sent a holy priest, St. John Eudes, to be the Father, the Doctor and the Apostle of this sweet devotion and to be the Author of the liturgical worship of the Sacred Hearts of Jesus and Mary.[1] Subsequently, he chose a holy Visitation nun, St. Margaret Mary Alacoque, to be the instrument in the hands of Divine Providence for the world-wide diffusion of this devotion and for the establishment in the universal Church of the Feast of the Sacred Heart. Today, devotion to the Sacred Heart of Jesus flourishes everywhere. Millions of Catholics find strength and comfort in its practice. The Church bestows rich blessings on all who participate therein and day by day more and more souls are drawn to share in the exercise of this beautiful and consoling devotion.

The book which is here presented in English dress was written in French by that great servant of God, St. John Eudes, to whose zeal and holiness and learning we owe the origins of the public worship of the Sacred Heart, and I deem it a high privilege to have the honor of introducing it to the reader.

[1] Pope Leo XIII, in declaring the heroism of the virtues of Father Eudes by the Papal Decree (Jan. 6, 1903) which proclaimed him "Venerable," bestowed upon him the title of "*Auctor liturgici cultus SS. Cordium Jesu et Mariae,*" and Pope Pius X, in the Decree of Beatification (April 25, 1909) pronounced Father Eudes "*Hujus suavissimae religionis tum Pater . . . tum Doctor . . . tum denique Apostolus.*"

The task of rendering into lucid and idiomatic English the rich prose of St. John Eudes without sacrificing either the simplicity of his language, the peculiar flavor of his seventeenth-century French, or the unction of his literary style presents a problem before which any translator might reasonably hesitate.

Dom Richard Flower, however, has courageously faced and overcome the difficulties of his task. His translation is smooth and easy, unencumbered by such obvious gallicisms as mar many translations, too hurriedly made, of notable French works. At the same time his choice of words remains as faithful to the letter of his original as is compatible with clear and correct English.

The rhythmical and rimed translations of the Sequence of the Mass in honor of the Sacred Heart and the Hymns of the Divine Office (printed at the end of this book) have been done with grace and skill. They truly preserve and reflect the spirit of St. John Eudes' strong but sensitive Latin poetry.

Throughout the long history of Christian worship, the Holy Ghost has enkindled in the hearts of the faithful many beautiful forms of piety and devotion. Each one of them, in its own peculiar way, opens up fresh vistas into "the depth of the riches of the wisdom and of the knowledge of God." [2] Each taps fresh sources of spiritual nourishment within the boundless treasure of grace and light and love stored up for us in the mysteries of religion.

Every new insight into the dealings of God with man, every new vision of His "incomprehensible judgments," [3] every new revelation of his "unsearchable ways," [4] brings to the mind fresh floods of light, stirs the soul to new transports of praise and love, arouses in the heart a deeper sense of man's unworthiness, his coldness and ingratitude towards "the Giver of all good gifts." [5] Gradually each of these aspects of the goodness and mercy of God becomes the focus of particular acts of piety and a special devotion arises to urge the soul onward to still greater generosity in the service of our loving Master.

[2] Rom. 11, 33.
[3] Ibid.
[4] Ibid.
[5] James 1, 17.

As a rule, it takes a long time for a new form of devotion to develop to the fulness of its beneficent power. Often it begins in some special insight of faith and fresh favor of love granted by the Holy Ghost to certain privileged souls. They perceive, in the light of God's wisdom and love, some new manifestation of His holy designs within this or that event of the life of Jesus Christ (whose special significance had hitherto passed unnoticed), or in some mystery of revealed truth (whose depths can never be plumbed), or in some word or deed recorded in the deposit of divine revelation (in which no one had previously noted this particular meaning and import). This fresh vision of the wisdom and love of God becomes for them a spur to some special devotion, appropriate to the grace and insight granted to them by the Holy Spirit. They begin to practise this new devotion in their private exercises of piety and find therein an increase of spiritual strength and courage, solace, comfort and love in the pursuit of Christian perfection.

Little by little the new devotion spreads. Other pious persons adopt its practice. It springs up here and there in various forms, not all of them alike and some of them, indeed, at times quite incompatible with others. And so it develops; while its object, aim and purpose become increasingly clear, its connection with some truth revealed by God more patently evident and its basis in Christian doctrine more firmly established. For, every devotion in the Church has some definite object and end; and all must rest upon the solid ground of dogmatic truth.

Only the revealed word of God, contained in the Holy Scriptures and Tradition, the deposit of Christian Faith which the Apostles bequeathed to the Church, can provide an adequate foundation for Christian worship. The extraordinary piety of individual souls, the holy inspirations which the Spirit of God so lavishly bestows upon all men, especially upon those who seek with all their hearts to reach the heights of Christian perfection, the special revelations which God vouchsafes to make from time to time to those chosen ones who are His special and particular friends, whether in the Person of our Blessed Lord Himself or through His holy Mother or His angels and His saints—even these exalted privileges and unusual signs of

divine favor—cannot furnish a sufficient reason or provide an adequate motive for the establishment of a special devotion as a part of
the public worship of the faithful, much as they may serve to in-
itiate the process of its development, accelerate its progress or occasion
its final acceptance and approval by the Church. But when some holy
and learned man of God arises and gathers together the scattered
traditions of past ages, sifts them out, studies their implications, finds
their roots in the revealed word of God, and proceeds systematically
to expound the theological justification for the special devotion in
question, then the way is at last prepared for official action by the
competent ecclesiastical authority. Once this official approval is
granted, the hitherto private devotion becomes part of the public
worship of the Church, an authorized liturgical cult.

The highest authority in this matter has always been, of course,
that of the Supreme Head of the Church, our Holy Father the Pope.
According to an ancient custom, however,—a custom which per-
sisted well on into the eighteenth century in many countries, notably
in France—the local Ordinary was wont to approve and sanction,
for his own diocese, the introduction of new feasts into the liturgy.
This widespread practice was supported both by the common opinion
of learned theologians and the authority of many prelates, saints and
doctors, while the Holy See allowed it to continue without protest.
Subsequently, indeed, it became clearly established that such innova-
tions could be sanctioned only by the supreme authority of the Vicar
of Christ. Certain feasts, therefore, which had theretofore been
authorized by episcopal decree alone afterwards received the approval
and sanction of the Holy See and were thus officially given the stand-
ing which they had long enjoyed by established custom and practice
and by the tacit approval of the Supreme Pontiff.

Today, it is universally recognized and acknowledged that the only
competent authority for the adoption of new feasts into the Liturgy
of the Church is the Pope. Normally the Holy Father acts in these
matters through the medium of the Sacred Congregation of Rites
which was established in the latter half of the sixteenth century. In
the usual course of the exercise of this authority, a new feast is at first
approved for certain definite localities—dioceses, missionary regions,

religious orders or congregations, pious or charitable institutions. Only later, when evidence is forthcoming that the faithful and the hierarchy earnestly desire and urgently plead for its extension to the universal Church, does the Holy See sanction its celebration throughout the whole world.

In its growth and development, the cult of the Sacred Heart of Jesus has followed the broad outlines of this historical pattern. From the earliest times the faithful looked upon the love of God, made abundantly manifest in the Incarnation of the Son of God and the Redemption of mankind upon the Cross, as the central element, the very core, of all Christian devotion. The spontaneous response which the Holy Ghost stirred up in the souls of pious persons in answer to that unspeakable, infinite, divine love expressed itself in an ardent love of the Christian soul for Jesus Christ and in the love of all Christians for one another and for all men for the love and sake of Christ. These two elements—the love of God for man and the reciprocal love of man for God—have always been present in the devotions of Christian people. They were destined to enter in a very special manner into the theory and practice of the worship of the Sacred Heart of Jesus.

Moreover, the metaphorical significance of the term "heart" as the figurative expression of "love" has been at all times a familiar notion in the history of Christian worship, as indeed it has been from time immemorial a commonly accepted figure of speech in the language and literature of men. "To give one's heart" has ever been synonymous with "to give one's love." Yet in the early centuries of Christian devotion there is no trace of the complicated symbolical meaning later perceived in the use of this term and there is no indication that the Heart of Jesus was especially reverenced as the symbol or the seat of the love of Jesus Christ either for His Heavenly Father or for mankind. This was to come only much later in history, when the sacred humanity of Christ began to be the object of particular homage.

Likewise, the faithful followers of Christ realized from very early times that the piercing of the sacred side of Jesus on the Cross by the lance of Longinus bore a deep and mysterious meaning, far beyond the mere physical act of a public executioner to assure himself that his victim is dead. For a long time, however, the mystic significance of this event was associated only with the origin of the Church of Christ. Just as Eve, the spouse of Adam, had come forth from the side of her husband when God had cast a deep sleep upon him, so the Church, the Spouse of Christ, issued from His sacred wounded side when He had slept in death; for, from the sacred side of Jesus wounded by the lance there gushed forth blood and water, symbols of the origin of the Church of Christ and the fulness of redemption and grace which flowed from His Passion and death upon the souls of men ransomed by His Precious Blood and washed in the waters of Baptism. Thus too, the wounding of the heart referred to in the Song of Solomon—"vulnerasti cor meum," [6]—was thought of in this context as the love of Jesus Christ for His Holy Spouse, the Church.

All these elements of traditional piety and devotion existed in some form or another in practically every period of Christian worship, but only in a scattered, disconnected and unrelated fashion. They had to await a much later period to be gathered together in that marvelous synthesis of doctrine and piety, the Devotion to the Sacred Heart of Jesus, which, in the words of Cardinal Pie, "is the very quintessence of Christianity and the substantial summary and compendium of all religion." [7] It would be vain, therefore, as Dom Berliere aptly remarks, to seek any trace of the Devotion to the Sacred Heart in the early centuries of the Church.[8] The spiritual element of the love of God and the metaphorical significance of the heart, figuratively expressing love, were indeed there; but that does not constitute devotion to the Sacred Heart of Jesus. There is as yet no mention of the union of that divine love of God with the burning love of soul of our Blessed Lord, expressed and symbolized in His Heart of flesh which beat within His sacred bosom and poured forth the last drop of Its Precious Blood upon the Cross for the salvation

---

[6] Canticle 4, 9.

[7] Cardinal Pie, *Oeuvres Episcopales*, 3:37.

[8] Dom Ursmer Berliere, *La Dévotion au Sacré Coeur dans l'ordre de St. Benoît* (Paris, 1923), p. 3.

of men. Yet, in the perspective of history, all these profound insights and tender effusions of love which characterized the devotions of pious Christians in ages past foreshadowed the formal devotion to the Sacred Heart as we know and love and practise it today.

These early adumbrations of this tender devotion gave place a little later to a somewhat clearer light. This came with the origin and spread of devotion to the sacred wounds of our Blessed Lord, especially to the wound in His sacred side. Many holy souls found a rich source of grace and consolation in the Devotion to the Five Wounds. For, as St. Gregory the Great had said, "Just as the dove finds nourishment in hollow places, so the simple soul seeks in the wounds of Christ the food that makes it strong." [9] St. Bernard and St. Francis of Assisi did much to propagate this form of devotion to the sacred body of Christ and the holy nuns, St. Mechtilde and St. Gertrude—whose influence was so strong in developing the devotion to the Sacred Heart—made frequent reference in their writings to the salutary power of devotion to the wounds of Christ.

The wound made by the lance in the sacred side of Jesus gradually became the object of a special and very popular devotion. As we look back over the historical evolution of Christian worship, this may well be regarded as the first stage in the development of Devotion to the Sacred Heart of Jesus. "Tardily, and as it were by a sudden enlightenment," says Dom Gougaud, "the thought of the Fathers of the Church was drawn towards the Wounded Heart of Jesus. Medieval contemplatives and masters of the spiritual life began timidly to turn thither their own devotion and to guide the devotion of chosen souls in this direction."[10] In the Middle Ages, mystics, theologians, directors of souls frequently and eloquently extol the merits and advantages of devotion to the wounded Heart of Jesus and record innumerable instances of great spiritual rewards granted to those who practise it.

From that period onward, devotion to the Sacred Heart became a favorite devotion for many privileged souls and their number

[9] Migne, *Comm. in Cant. Canticor*, P.L. 79:499.
[10] Dom G. Gougaud, "Le coeur vulnéré du Sauveur," *Vie et Arts Liturgiques,* Mars, 1921, p. 198.

steadily increased. Although its devotees were quite aware that the object of their devotion was the Sacred Heart of Jesus and although their homage and love were consciously directed to the Sacred Heart of Jesus, the practice of the devotion nevertheless most frequently appeared in connection with some other devotion, for instance, devotion to the Passion, the Five Wounds, the sacred body of Jesus pierced with the lance, or the Blessed Eucharist, from which it was not as yet clearly and definitely distinguished. Gradually, however, Devotion to the Sacred Heart developed still further in clarity and distinctness until, even before the lifetime of St. John Eudes, it had become known and was practised by many holy persons. St. Bonaventure, the holy nuns of Helfta, St. Mechtilde and St. Gertrude, the pious Carthusian monk, Lanspergius, the Venerable Abbot Louis of Blois and many others had shed great light upon the theory and practice of the devotion and St. John Eudes drew heavily upon their store of wisdom and piety in elaborating his doctrine and method of devotion to the Sacred Heart. Up to this time, however, it was still a private devotion with no special form of its own, no generally accepted mode of practice and no authorized method. Above all, no ecclesiastical authority had as yet given it formal and official approval. Its general character, although greatly clarified over the passing years, had not yet become quite definite and clear because nobody had accurately set forth in due theological form its proper, specific object, its distinctive end and purpose, its doctrinal foundation and the exact method of its practice.

It was the divinely appointed mission of St. John Eudes (for, as His Holiness, Pope Pius X has declared, St. John Eudes did not enter upon his work without divine inspiration) to inaugurate in the Church the public worship of the Sacred Heart. That mission could not have been accomplished, however, until he had first established the theological soundness of the devotion, defined its precise object, and provided a suitable liturgical Office and Mass for the proper celebration of the Feast of the Sacred Heart. These tasks he undertook with characteristic courage, zeal and learning. Moreover, the tireless energy he expended in propagating this most tender and salutary devotion not only resulted in spreading far and wide a clearer understanding of its aim and object but also deepened, developed, and spread its regular and formal practice among great multitudes of the faithful. At long last, the Devotion to the Sacred Heart was firmly established. To this great saint we owe the first public celebration of the Feast of the Sacred Heart in the liturgy of the Church. The heroic sanctity of his own personal life, his zeal for the establishment and propagation of his cherished devotion, his fruitful apostolate in its behalf, his great learning and piety, displayed both in the composition of his liturgical Offices and Masses in honor of the admirable Heart of Mary and the Sacred Heart of Jesus and in his enlightened exposition and defense of the doctrinal foundations of this form of devotion and worship gained for St. John Eudes the honors of the altar as well as high titles of praise and reverence from the Sovereign Pontiffs who declared him Venerable, Blessed and Saint.

It is popularly believed that Devotion to the Sacred Heart of Jesus originated with the revelations which our Blessed Lord granted to St. Margaret Mary Alacoque and that the Venerable Claude de la Colombière, St. Margaret Mary's spiritual director, was the first to preach that devotion to the people. But this is not true. What is true, however, is that the enormous importance of the mission which St. Margaret Mary received from our Lord Himself and the great zeal with which Father de la Colombière and many other priests of the Society of Jesus labored to fulfil the express desires of the Sacred Heart for spread of this devotion to the universal Church have unduly obscured the rôle of St. John Eudes as the Father, Doctor and Apostle of this beautiful devotion.

St. John Eudes had practised and preached devotion to the Sacred Heart for many years before Our Lord appeared to St. Margaret Mary. In fact, his zealous work had gone so far forth before that date, that the Office and Mass which he had composed in honor of the Sacred Heart received ecclesiastical approval some years before St. Margaret Mary entered the Convent of the Visitation, and the Feast of the Sacred Heart was publicly established and celebrated in several dioceses a year or so before the first of those marvelous apparitions of Our Lord to His holy and humble servant, St. Margaret Mary.

Nor was the character of the devotion, which St. John Eudes had preached, altered by the revelations made to this saintly nun. For, the Mass in honor of the Sacred Heart which St. John Eudes had composed and in which his teaching on the nature and purpose of devotion to the Sacred Heart is gloriously enshrined, was adopted for the celebration of the Feast prescribed by our Blessed Lord in one of His revelations to St. Margaret Mary and continued to be used even in convents of the Visitation Nuns for at least fifty years after the death of St. Margaret Mary.

Although St. John Eudes has been honored by the supreme authority of the Holy See with the enviable titles of "Author of the Liturgical Worship of the Sacred Hearts of Jesus and Mary" and "The Father, The Doctor and The Apostle of this devotion," surprisingly few persons are aware of the decisive part he played in establishing and propagating the now widespread Devotion to the Sacred Heart. Yet it was he who, inspired by the Holy Ghost, first thought of rendering public worship by a special liturgical Office and Mass to the Sacred Heart of Jesus. It was he who inaugurated many solemn festivals in honor of the Sacred Heart, first in the institutions conducted by the religious communities of which he was the founder, namely, The Congregation of Jesus and Mary (Eudist Fathers) and the Order of Our Lady of Charity (Good Shepherd Nuns), and subsequently, with the approval of the hierarchy, in various dioceses of Normandy and Brittany. It was he who composed the Office and Mass to which these bishops gave their whole-hearted approval. It was he who laid firm the theological foundations upon which Devotion to the Sacred Heart, like all devotions of the Church, remains so solidly grounded. It was he who expounded and defended the doctrine and practice of Devotion to the Sacred Heart against its earliest adversaries. It was he who labored all his life long with unflagging zeal and notable success to spread Devotion to the Sacred Heart by his preaching, through his writings, in his missions, by his personal exhortation and example and by the founding of pious confraternities whose members dedicated themselves in a special manner to the practice and propagation of the Devotion to the Sacred Heart. Upon these pious associations the Holy See showered its choicest favors and blessings, enriching the practice of the devotion cultivated by them with numerous and precious indulgences.

When all this labor of love had been accomplished and the ground so well prepared for world-wide acceptance of this highly important devotion, our Blessed Lord appeared to the holy Visitation nun, St. Margaret Mary Alacoque, and confided to her the desires of His most Sacred Heart. Jesus Christ Himself picked this saintly religious to be the divinely appointed instrument for the diffusion of devotion to His Sacred Heart throughout the length and breadth of Christendom, to be the privileged depository of those heavenly promises made by our Blessed Lord Himself in favor of all who love and practise this devotion, to be the providential means of establishing the Feast of the Sacred Heart to be celebrated on the Friday following the Octave of the Feast of Corpus Christi throughout the universal Church.

By the time the extraordinary favors which the Sacred Heart of Jesus had bestowed upon St. Margaret Mary became generally known and the revelations and promises made to her were made public, St. John Eudes had passed to his eternal reward. His work had been accomplished and his labors ended. The Office and Mass he had composed in honor of the Sacred Heart was already incorporated into the liturgy and the soil had been prepared by his apostolic zeal for the diffusion throughout the whole world of the devotion he so ardently loved. From that time onward the mission of St. Margaret Mary became the decisive factor in the spread of devotion to the Sacred Heart. The saint herself did not live to see the fulfilment of that mission, but the efforts of all those who espoused the holy cause (especially the work of Father de la Columbière and many other priests of the Society of Jesus) were at last crowned with success and the Sacred Heart finally conquered the whole world.

In the fulness and fervor of our gratitude to our dear Lord for having disclosed the love of His most Sacred Heart by means of special revelations made to His servant, St. Margaret Mary Alacoque, it behooves us to remember with equal fulness and fervor of gratitude the less striking, though not less important, mission which He deigned to confide to the great saint to whose zeal and learning the Church owes the origin of the public worship of the Sacred Heart of Jesus, the demonstration of its doctrinal stability, the statement of its theological justification and the earliest diffusion of its practice. It is but just that due honor be paid to all whom God has chosen to be His instruments in the glorious work of establishing and propagating the worship and love of the Sacred Heart of His Divine Son. It cannot detract from the honor due to St. Margaret Mary to confess and proclaim with the Holy See the honor due to that other holy servant of God, St. John Eudes. We should join with St. Margaret Mary herself and with all those good priests who helped to further the explicit desires of the Sacred Heart and who, please God, are with her now in heaven, in gratefully acknowledging and rejoicing in the privilege which Jesus Christ our Lord has bestowed upon St. John Eudes in deigning to make use of his mind and heart, his tongue and pen, to set up in the Church and spread abroad the public worship of His most Sacred Heart.

From early childhood, St. John Eudes had cherished a tender devotion to our Blessed Lady, a devotion which grew more intense and deeper through all the years of his long life. Only in his young manhood, after reading St. Mechtilde and St. Gertrude, did he begin to practise Devotion to the Sacred Heart. In his early work, *The Life and the Kingdom of Jesus,* we find unmistakable traces of what was later to become the full picture of this devotion which was drawn with the bold firm strokes of his learned pen in the twelfth book of his monumental work, *Le Coeur Admirable de la Très Sacrée Mère de Dieu.* It is this book which is here published in English translation.

Mary had led St. John Eudes to Jesus. And in Jesus he found Mary more glorious, more lovable, more admirable than ever. That is why, in the thoughts and affections of St. John Eudes Mother and Son are never separated. The love he praises in the most pure Heart of Mary is the love of Jesus Himself; and he sings with one single hymn, *Ave, Cor Sanctissimum,* the love of the admirable Heart of Mary and the love of the adorable Heart of Jesus. This does not indicate, as some have thought, a certain confusion in his mind regarding the Devotion to the Sacred Heart. On the contrary, it manifests a penetrating insight into the deepest meaning of the devotion and a profound appreciation of the mystery of sanctification, the mystery of that union in love which transforms the soul and makes it one with God. St. John Eudes was keenly aware of the infinite difference between the honor due to Mary, the Mother of God (in whom the love of Jesus, though shared in the plenitude of creaturely capacity, was still a gratuitous gift of God), and the supreme honor due to her Divine Son (in whom the fullness of the Godhead dwells and whose love is God's subsistent and eternal love, in which Our Lady shares). Even while his thoughts were occupied with establishing the cult of the admirable Heart of Mary, his plans were maturing for the writing of his treatise and his meditations on the Sacred Heart of Jesus and for the composition of his Office and Mass in honor of the adorable Heart of our divine Lord.

Although the book he wrote on *The Devotion to the Sacred Heart of Jesus* is not now extant, and perhaps was never published, the section of his writings which is here presented in English contains the substance of his teaching on the subject. It is the first theological treatise ever written on Devotion to the Sacred Heart and, when read in conjunction with the Office and Mass of the Sacred Heart which St. John Eudes composed and with appropriate passages in the earlier sections of this same great work, *Le Coeur Admirable*, provides as profound and exact a study of the theology of the Sacred Heart as has ever been produced. Certain expressions which St. John Eudes uses to convey his ideas are no longer in current usage but the doctrine expounded in this work has stood the test of time. Many learned writers would have saved themselves much labor in developing the theory of the devotion to the Sacred Heart and not a few historians of the devotion would have been spared undue mistakes had they given more careful attention to this work.

For St. John Eudes, as for all Catholics, the ultimate object of all devotion is God, in the unity of His divine nature and in the Trinity of His Persons. But God sent His Only-begotten Son to redeem and save mankind from the penalty of sin. Through Jesus Christ our Lord and Saviour and through Him alone can we mortals have access to divinity. All the religious life of Christians is, therefore, centered in the Word of God made Flesh. Yet it extends to all Three Persons of the Blessed Trinity and, by participation, to all persons, places and things made holy unto God.

The worship of the Incarnate Word embraces all that Jesus is in Himself—His divine nature and His sacred humanity—and to all He does in heaven, on earth and in hell, whilst the homage which is offered through any and every act of worship is directed to the Person of the Word. Whence, in virtue of the hypostatic union of the divine and human natures in Christ, every part and every perfection of the being and the life of Jesus Christ may be made the object of a special devotion provided only that it be not separated from the Person of the Incarnate Word. Jesus is adorable in Himself and in all the mysteries of His existence, in all the perfections of His divine and human natures, in His human soul, with all its powers, faculties and virtues, in His human body, with all its parts and organs, in all His thoughts and words and deeds. Above all, Jesus is adorable in the love He bears to His Heavenly Father, in the love He bestows upon His holy Mother and in the love He lavishes on all His creatures.

But Jesus is both God and Man. Being very God, He loves His Heavenly Father with an infinite and eternal love and He loves us, too, from all eternity with that uncreated love which moved Him to become Man to save us from perdition and to fill our souls with His divine life and love. Being very man, He loves us with all the fervor of His most perfect soul, a human love so tender and so strong, so ardent and so full, that no other human love could be conceived to be so great. The uncreated love of God, which is the principle and source of Christ's created human love and that human love itself, more powerful than any love mere man could ever cherish, reverberate within the Heart of Flesh which throbs within His sacred bosom and adds the human glow of purest passion and emotion to all that great torrent of love which flows from all eternity, through time and unto everlasting.

It is this immense and ineffable love of Jesus Christ in all its aspects and in all its phases which is the specific object of Devotion to the Sacred Heart.

St. John Eudes had gleaned from his prayerful study of Holy Writ many meanings given by the inspired writers to the word, *heart*. He found the word sometimes referred to the material, corporeal organ which we bear in our breasts; sometimes it was used to signify the memory, the understanding or the will; again, it meant the highest point of the soul, the *apex mentis* of patristic and mediae-val writers, the seat of contemplation or even the whole interior of man; finally, the Holy Ghost was referred to as the "new spirit" and the "new heart" which God would fain give to men and the Son of God Himself was called the Heart of the Eternal Father.

All these meanings St. John Eudes gathered up into one theory which embraced them all. For him, the Sacred Heart of Jesus was the synthesis of (a) the divine, uncreated love of Jesus Christ (i.e., the *essential* love of God, common to all Three Divine Persons of the Most Holy Trinity; the *notional* love of God, the reciprocal love of God the Father and God the Son from which the Holy Ghost proceeds; the *personal* love of God which is the Divine Person of the Holy Ghost Himself); (b) the human love of Jesus proceeding from His human will and affecting concomitantly all the higher powers of His soul; and (c) the sensible, passionate, emotional love of Jesus, symbolized by the Heart of Flesh, the seat of the emotions, and which St. John Eudes also regarded as the organ of the passions.

To designate this threefold object of the devotion to the Sacred Heart, St. John Eudes distinguished three Hearts in Jesus, namely, *His divine Heart* (indicating His uncreated love), *His spiritual Heart* (indicating the love of His soul, His human will and higher faculties), and *His corporeal Heart* (indicating the echo of love in the bodily organ which is its symbol and the seat of its emotional warmth). These expressions are no longer in use but they convey a doc-trine which has not been altered with the ages. St. John Eudes hastens to add that these three Hearts are but one absolutely single Heart, filled with infinite love for the Holy Trinity and inconceivable charity for mankind; for, he says, the divine Heart of Jesus is the soul, the life and the heart of both His spiritual Heart and His corporeal Heart.

The aim and purpose of Devotion to the Sacred Heart are to in-flame our hearts with a reciprocal love of Jesus and to stir up in our souls appropriate acts of adoration, thanksgiving, repentance and peti-tion enlivened by that love. For, the Sacred Heart of Jesus is a "flaming furnace of love" which, like a burning fire, seeks to enkindle in our souls an ardent flame of love and to transform them with its all consuming power. Father Bainvel has well said, "The whole Devotion to the Sacred Heart can be summed up in this: on the one side, a love which calls for love, a tender, overflowing love which calls for a proportionate love; on the other side, a love which answers the call of love, a love concerned not to fall too far short of the immense love which has anticipated and aroused it." This is the doctrine of St. John Eudes as may be clearly seen in the pages that follow. In this fashion he understood those powerful words of our Blessed Lord, "I am come to cast fire on the earth. And what will I, but that it be kindled." [11]

Every act of devotion to the Sacred Heart of Jesus must be enlivened by this all-pervading spirit of love. St. John Eudes sums up under four general headings the appropriate acts which constitute the practice of this devotion. First, to adore the Sacred Heart of Jesus. Secondly, to praise, bless, glorify and thank Him for His love. Thirdly, to ask pardon for our offenses against His great love and to make reparation for them. Fourthly, to love Him in return for all His love and beg Him to establish within our hearts the reign of His Holy love.

In the concluding words of that beautiful prayer, *Ave, Cor Sanctissimum,* composed by St. John Eudes and prescribed by him for daily recitation in the religious communities he founded, these acts, proper to the devotion to the Sacred Heart, are set forth with unusual fervor and unction. This prayer teaches us that the Sacred Heart must be adored, praised and glorified in all His manifestations of love. With our whole hearts, with our whole strength and with all our minds we must return this love. To Him we offer, dedicate, consecrate and immolate our hearts that He may wholly take and possess them, live and reign in them now and always, forever and forever.

The contemplation of the love of the Sacred Heart of Jesus for His Heavenly Father, for His Blessed Mother, for all members of His Church Triumphant, Suffering and Militant, constitutes the deepest foundation of devotion to the Sacred Heart. Upon this foundation St.

[11] Luke 12, 49.

John Eudes builds the whole practice of the Devotion. From the contemplation of these great truths, he bids us pass to the consideration of what the love of God has done for each of us in particular by creating us, by redeeming us, by giving us the gift of divine grace and the promise of eternal reward. And, since that great love of the Sacred Heart of Jesus is especially manifest in the sufferings and death of Our Lord upon the Cross and in the Blessed Sacrament of the Eucharist, there exists a particularly cogent reason for practising the devotion to the Sacred Heart in and through devotion to the Passion of our Saviour and to the Most Holy Sacrament of the Altar.

The most striking characteristic of the teaching of St. John Eudes on Devotion to the Sacred Heart—as indeed of his whole teaching on the spiritual life—is that Christ is always its centre. Through Christ, with Christ, in Christ—*per Ipsum, cum Ipso et in Ipso*—all devotion and all piety achieves its end.

Since the Sacred Heart of Jesus is *God's Love* symbolically (though by no means merely metaphorically, figuratively or arbitrarily) expressed, all those acts which belong to strictly divine worship (*cultus latriae*) have first place in this devotion. For, God Himself is its object. But these acts, as such, are common to all forms of divine worship. In order to become part of a particular devotion they require to be specified by the formal aspect of the particular object which characterizes that devotion. In the Devotion to the Sacred Heart, this object is the love of the Word Made Flesh both for His Father in Heaven and for all men; and its end is to arouse in the hearts of all who practise it an ardent reciprocal love for Jesus Christ, the Incarnate Word of God. Thus all the particular acts appropriate to the practice of this devotion and to the achievement of its end and purpose must stem from the specific act which constitutes its proper act and marks it as a special and distinct devotion, namely, the act of love. The love of Jesus, symbolically expressed and most aptly conveyed by the phrase, "The Sacred Heart of Jesus," evokes a reciprocal love from the hearts of all men. All other acts which enter into the practice of this devotion flow from this, its proper act, and are instinct with the spirit which it breathes.

In the teaching of St. John Eudes, this order and balance among the various acts which constitute the method and practice of Devotion to the Sacred Heart are admirably maintained. And, although the Devotion, as preached and taught by St. John Eudes, is suffused with the tenderest affection and unction, this is always controlled by strict theological reason and never becomes purely sentimental or emotional. The acts of dedication, immolation, consecration and reparation each has its proper place within that order. They all form part of the full practice of the Devotion to the Sacred Heart, each in its proper proportion. All are dependent upon, and subordinate to, the specific act proper to this particular devotion, the act of love for the Sacred Heart of Jesus, which in turn is incorporated within the whole body of those acts of religion which belong to divine worship in its strictest form. In a word, the doctrine of St. John Eudes is unequivocally Christocentric.

The influence which, since the Renaissance, has tended to make human thought and life in all its phases, even in its spiritual and religious aspects, a man-centered life, is entirely absent from the spirit of St. John Eudes. Christ for him has been, is and always shall be the centre of our life, the focus of all our thoughts and words and deeds. "Christ yesterday, Christ today, Christ forever."

There are notable indications in the writings of scholars who are expert in the history and the theology of the Devotion to the Sacred Heart pointing towards a deeper and fuller understanding of the teaching of St. John Eudes. The contrasts which have at times been drawn between the devotion to the Sacred Heart as preached by St. John Eudes and as revealed to St. Margaret Mary Alacoque are being progressively revealed as historically and theologically indefensible. Please God, the time is not far off when the whole preaching and practice of the Devotion to the Sacred Heart will be consciously enlivened by the full theological spirit which St. John Eudes first infused into the great synthesis of doctrine which he elaborated as the basis of the public worship of the Sacred Heart of Jesus.

GERALD B. PHELAN

The Pontifical Institute of Mediaeval Studies,
Toronto, September 20, 1944.

THE SACRED HEART
OF JESUS

CHAPTER I

THE SACRED HEART OF JESUS IS A FURNACE OF BURNING LOVE FOR HIS ETERNAL FATHER

INNUMERABLE reasons urge us to offer our worship and honor to the Sacred Heart of our most adorable Saviour with extraordinary devotion and, reverence. All these reasons are embodied in the words of St. Bernardine of Siena, who calls this loving Heart: *Fornacem ardentissimae caritatis ad inflammandum et incendendum orbem universum.* "A furnace of ardent love to enkindle and inflame the whole universe."[1] Most certainly the admirable Heart of Jesus is a furnace of love for His Divine Father, for His Blessed Mother, and for His Church Triumphant, Militant and Suffering, and also for each one of us. This we shall see in the following chapters.

Let us consider, first of all, the most brilliant flames of this great furnace of love for the Eternal Father. What mind can conceive and what tongue express the tiniest spark of this illimitable flaming furnace of love for His Father? It is a love worthy of such a Father and of such a Son. It is a love that most perfectly equals the ineffable perfections of its beloved object. Here is a Son infinitely loving a Father who is infinitely lovable, a God loving a God. Here is love in its very essence loving eternal love: a love that is boundless, incomprehensible, infinite, passing all limits, and loving in turn a love that is boundless, incomprehensible, infinite, and passing all limits.

[1] Sermon 514, *de Passione Domini*, p. 2, tit. 1. In the picture called *Our Lady of Hearts* St. John Eudes represented the Sacred Hearts of Jesus and Mary by the emblem of a furnace of love, whither his disciples go to light torches to enkindle the universe. It is really but a beautiful application of the words of Our Lord in St. Luke 12, 49: "I am come to cast fire on the earth. And what will I, but that it be kindled?"

In a word, the Sacred Heart of Jesus, whether considered in His divinity or in His humanity, is more ardently enkindled with love for His Father, loving Him infinitely more at any given moment, than all the hearts of angels and saints together can love Him throughout all eternity.

There is no greater love than to give one's life for the person one loves. The Son of God so loves His Father that He would be ready to sacrifice His own life again, as He sacrificed it upon the Cross, and to sacrifice it by suffering the same torments for the love of His Father (if such were God's holy will) that He suffered on Calvary. Since His love is boundless, He would be ready to lay down His life throughout the whole universe as He did upon Calvary. Since His love is eternal and infinite, He would be ready to make this sacrifice over and over again, if it were possible, and with infinite suffering.

"O Divine Father, Creator, Preserver, and Ruler of the whole world, there is no one so lovable as Thou. Thy manifold and infinite perfections, and the unspeakable blessings Thou hast in store for all Thy creatures, place upon them endless obligations to serve, honor and love Thee with all their strength. Yet there is no one in the whole world who is so little loved as Thou, no one who is so scorned and insulted by most of Thy creatures. *Oderunt me et Patrem meum.* 'They have hated both me and my Father,'[2] Jesus Thy Son has said, 'without cause they have hated me. I have never done them any harm but have lavished on them all manner of good': *Odio habuerunt me gratis.*[3] I behold hell filled with an untold number of the damned, ceaselessly venting their multitudinous blasphemies against Thy divine majesty. I behold the earth filled with unbelievers, Jews, heretics, and false Christians who treat Thee as if Thou wert their archenemy.

"But two thoughts are my consolation and joy. The first is that Thy perfections and Thy splendors, O my God, are so admirable. Thou dost take so great a pleasure and so perfect a satisfaction in the infinite love of Thy Divine Son and in all that He hath suffered

[2] John 15, 24.
[3] John 15, 25.

with that infinite love, to repair the injuries that Thy enemies have striven and still strive to do Thee, that they have not been able or ever will be able to detract the least iota from Thy glory and Thy felicity.

"The second joyful thought is that Jesus, Thy Well-beloved Son, by His incomparable overflowing goodness willed to be our Head and chose us to be His members. He has associated us with Himself in His ineffable love for Thee. He has given us as a result the power to love Thee with the same love wherewith He loves Thee, with a love eternal, boundless, and infinite."

To understand this truth well, take note of three important facts. First, the love of the Son of God for His Heavenly Father, being eternal, does not pass away, but remains forever, stable and abiding. Secondly, the love of the Son of God for His Father fills all things by its immensity; consequently it abides in us and in our hearts: *Intimo meo intimior,* as St. Augustine says. Thirdly, as the Father of Jesus has given us all things in giving us His Son—*cum ipso omnia donavit* [4]—the love of the Son of God for the Father belongs to us, and we can and must make use of it as a possession that is ours. On this basis, I can, with my Saviour, love His Divine Father and mine, with the same love wherewith He loves Him; with a love which I can put into practice, thus:

"O my Saviour, I give myself to Thee to unite myself to Thy eternal, boundless, and infinite love for Thy Almighty Father. O Adorable Father, I offer Thee all the eternal, boundless, and infinite love of Thy Son Jesus as a love which is mine. Just as our lovable Saviour says to us: *Sicut dilexit me Pater, et ego dilexi vos,* 'As the Father hath loved me, I also love you,' [5] I may say to Thee: 'O Divine Father, I love Thee, even as Thy Son loveth Thee.' "

The Father's love for the Son is no less mine than the Son's love for the Father; therefore I can make use of it, thus:

"O Father of Jesus, I give myself to Thee to be united to Thy boundless and eternal love for Thy Beloved Son. O my Jesus, I offer Thee all the eternal, boundless, and infinite love of Thy Father, and

[4] Rom. 8, 32.
[5] John 15, 9.

I offer it to Thee as a love which is mine." In this way, as our loving
Redeemer says to us: 'I love you as my Father loveth me,' I can say
in turn to Him: 'I love Thee, my Saviour, as Thy Eternal Father
loveth Thee.' "

O ineffable goodness! O wondrous love! What bliss for us that
the Eternal Father gives us His Only-begotten Son, and with Him all
things else! He gives Him to us not only to be our Redeemer, our
Brother, and our Father, but also to be our Head. What a privilege
to be members of the Son of God, to be one with Him, as the members are one with the Head, hence to have but one spirit, one heart,
one love with Christ, and thus to be able to love His Divine Father,
and our Father, with one and the same Heart and love!

It is, therefore, not surprising that, speaking of us to His Heavenly
Father, Our Lord says: *Dilexisti eos sicut et me dilexisti,* "Thou hast
loved them as Thou hast also loved me," [6] and He implores Him to
love us always: *Dilectio, qua dilexisti me, in ipsis sit.*[7] If we love
the Father as His Son loves Him, He loves us as He loves His Divine
Son. He beholds us in His Son as members of Christ who are but
one with the Son and love the Father with the same filial love. Truly
He loves us with one and the same Heart and love wherewith He
loves His Son.

Would that heaven and earth and all creatures might be changed
into a pure flame of love for the Father of goodness and for the only
Son of His divine delight, as St. Paul calls him: *Transtulit nos in
regnum Filii dilectionis suae!*[8]

[6] John 17, 23.
[7] *Ibid.* 17, 26.
[8] Col. 1, 13.

CHAPTER 2

THE SACRED HEART OF JESUS IS A FURNACE OF ARDENT LOVE FOR HIS MOST HOLY MOTHER

NOTHING IS easier than the proof of this truth. The ineffable graces with which our Saviour endowed His Blessed Mother clearly manifest that His love for her is a love without measure or limit. She is, after His Divine Father, the first and most worthy object of His love. He loves her incomparably more than all His angels, saints and other creatures together. The extraordinary favors with which He honored her and the wonderful privileges He conferred upon her, far beyond any other creature, are clear proofs of this truth. Let us examine these numerous and impressive privileges.

First of all, the Blessed Virgin is the only human being whom the Son of God chose from all eternity to elevate above all created things, to set on the highest throne of glory and grandeur, and to adorn with the most admirable of all dignities, the Motherhood of God.

Let us descend in spirit from eternity to the fulness of time, and we shall see this hallowed Virgin alone among the children of Adam in her preservation from original sin, through a very special privilege, in. testimony of which Holy Church celebrates annually throughout the world the Feast of her Immaculate Conception.

Not only did the love of God's Son for His most holy Mother preserve her from original sin, but over and above that, He filled her from the moment of her conception with such eminent grace that, according to several great theologians, it surpassed the grace of the chief of the Seraphim and of the greatest of all the saints even taken in its perfection. She alone among all the children of Adam enjoyed this privilege.

Moreover, from the first moment of her existence, she possessed the privilege of the light of reason and faith, by which she began to know God, to adore Him, and to give herself to Him. In virtue of another privilege she alone began to love God from the initial moment of her life, and she loved Him more ardently than the most flaming of the Seraphim. She alone loved Him continuously, incessantly, throughout the whole course of her life. For this reason we say that her life was one single act of love from the first to the last moment, an act that was never interrupted.

She is the only creature who has always perfectly accomplished the first of the divine commandments: "Thou shalt love the Lord thy God with thy whole heart, with thy whole soul, and with all thy strength." [1] Hence several Doctors of the Church assert that her love was doubled with each hour, or even, according to some, with each moment. When a soul makes an act of love with his whole heart and according to the whole extent of the grace within him, his love becomes twice as great as it was before. The Blessed Virgin loved God continuously with all her heart and all her strength. If she had ten degrees of love at the first instant of her life, she had twenty at the second; if she had twenty at the second, she had forty at the third. Thus her love was doubled every moment or at least every hour throughout the course of her life. You can imagine, therefore, what a furnace and what fires of divine love inflamed that virginal heart in the last days of her abode upon earth.

Let us pass on to the consideration of the matchless privileges by which the Only Son of Mary enriched His holy Mother. According to several eminent Doctors, He gave to her alone the grace to merit, by her prayers and tears, the accomplishment of His Incarnation. She alone gave human flesh, from her own substance, to Him who was born from all eternity in the bosom of God of the substance of the Father. Yes, Mary gave a portion of her virginal substance and of her most pure blood to fashion the sacred humanity of the Son of God. In addition, she cooperated with the Father, the Son, and the Holy Ghost in the union which was formed of her substance with the Person of the Son of God. Thus she participated in the accom-

[1] Deut. 6, 5.

plishment of the mystery of the Incarnation, and consequently in the greatest miracle that God ever has or ever will or even ever can perform.

There is another privilege that contributes to the matchless honor of Our Lady. The most pure blood and the virginal flesh which she offered for this mystery will remain united forever, by the hypostatic union, to the Person of the Incarnate Word. The virginal blood and the precious flesh of Mary are, therefore, to be adored in the humanity of the Son of God with the same adoration that is due to that very humanity itself, and they will be forever the object of the adoration of all the angels and saints. O incomparable privilege! O ineffable love of Jesus for His most holy Mother!

There are still other prerogatives. That loving Mother also gave the flesh and blood from which the adorable Heart of the Child Jesus was formed. The Sacred Heart of the Son of God received its nourishment and its increase from that same blood, during the nine months of its abode in the holy womb of the Blessed Virgin.

The incomparable Virgin is alone in occupying the place of father and mother in respect to the God-Man, and hence in having paternal and maternal authority over Him, and in receiving the honor of being obeyed by the Sovereign of the Universe, an honor that is greater than she would receive from the homage of all created beings.

She alone is Mother and Virgin together, and according to some holy Doctors she made the vow of virginity from the moment of her Immaculate Conception. She alone bore in her womb for nine months Him whom the Eternal Father embraces in His bosom for all eternity. She alone gave life to Him who is eternal life and who gives life to all living things.

Accompanied by St. Joseph, she abode with that adorable Saviour for the space of thirty years. O wondrous thing! Our divine Redeemer came upon earth to save mankind. Yet He set aside only three years and three months of His life for the work of preaching and instructing. The other thirty years He devoted to the ever-increasing sanctification of His holy Mother. What a wealth of graces and blessings He incessantly poured into the soul of His Blessed Mother! With what flames of heavenly fire did the divine Heart of Jesus enkindle ever more and more the virgin Heart of His most worthy Mother, especially when those two Hearts were so close to each other and so firmly united, while she bore Him in her womb, nursed Him, and held Him in her arms; during the whole time that she lived with Him familiarly as a mother with her child, eating and drinking with Him, praying with Him, and hearing the divine words coming from His adorable lips as so many coals of fire ever enkindling more and more her most holy Heart with the sacred fire of divine love!

After this who can estimate how ardently the blessed Heart of the Mother of the Saviour was afire with love for God? Certainly there is great reason to believe that, if her Son had not miraculously preserved her until the decreed hour of death, she would have died of love, not only once, like St. Teresa, but a thousand times, since her love was immeasurably more than that of the great Carmelite mystic. From earliest childhood her love was sufficiently intense to have caused her death and, when her Beloved Son did call her, she died of love that He might give her, after His own, the happiest and most glorious life possible.

Let us repeat concerning the marvelous Virgin that she is the only one, after her Divine Son, to have been transported body and soul into heaven. In accordance with the tradition of Holy Church, Mary's Assumption is solemnly celebrated throughout the world. She alone is raised on high above all the choirs of angels and saints and sits at the right hand of her Son. She alone is crowned Queen of heaven and earth, of angels and men, the Sovereign Empress of the universe. She alone has all power over the Church Triumphant, Militant, and Suffering. *In Jerusalem potestas mea.*[2] She alone has more influence with her Divine Son Jesus than all the citizens of heaven together: *Data est tibi omnis potestas in caelo et in terra,* says St. Peter Damian.

There is yet another particular privilege, emphasized in these words of St. Anselm: *Te, Domina, tacente, nullus orabit, nullus adjuvabit; te autem orante, omnes (nempe Sancti) orabunt, omnes adjuvabunt:* "O my Queen, if thou prayest not for anyone or for anything, no

[2] Eccles. 24, 15.

one shall proffer help, but when thou prayest all the saints pray with thee, all the saints put forth their aid."

Is it not true then that here is a great number of privileges and advantages with which our Saviour has honored His most holy Mother? What has constrained Him to do so? The burning love with which His filial Heart is all on fire for her. Why does He love her so much?

1. She is His Mother, from whom He received a new being and a new life by the new birth which she gave Him on earth.

2. He loves her alone more than He loves all creatures together because she loves Him more than all created things.

3. He loves her most ardently because she cooperated with Him in the accomplishment of His great work of the Redemption of the world. Her cooperation was to give Him a mortal body capable of suffering and of sustaining the torments of His Passion. She also imparted to Him the Precious Blood which He shed for us, and she offered that body, that blood, and that life as a sacrifice at the foot of the Cross.

As our Saviour's love for His Blessed Mother is so great, we must be obliged to love and serve her to the best of our ability. Let us then love her with her Son Jesus, and if we love them let us hate what they hate and love what they love. Let us have but one heart with them, a heart detesting what they detest, that is, sin, especially the sins against charity, humility and purity, and a heart that loves what they love, particularly the poor, all Christian virtues, and trials. O Mother of goodness, obtain for us these graces from Thy Son!

CHAPTER 3

THE SACRED HEART OF JESUS HAS ENDOWED HIS BLESSED MOTHER WITH WONDROUS AUTHORITY AND POWER IN HEAVEN

LET US ADD to the foregoing privileges still another prerogative, the greatest of all. It is this: the Mother of God is eternally associated in heaven not only with the highest authority of the Eternal Father, His adorable paternity, but likewise she possesses the authority of the Mother of the Divine Son as on earth: *Et erat subditus illis.*[1] This is a greater glory for her than if she exercised power over a million worlds. Her Son infinitely surpasses her in glory, power and majesty; yet He will eternally look upon her and honor her as His real Mother. His place as Son of God, says St. Ambrose, did not dispense Him while on earth from the divine and natural obligation which He had like all other children of obeying His Mother, according to the words: *Et erat subditus illis.* This submission was to Him not a matter of shame but rather of honor and glory; it was voluntary and proceeded not from weakness but from filial devotion: *Non utique infirmitatis,* as this holy Father declares, *est ista subjectio, sed pietatis.*

Several eminent theologians are agreed that the Mother of the Saviour had actual authority over the person of her Son, whether it was by a right of nature or by virtue of His goodness and humility. The greatest of all names that one can bestow upon the Blessed Virgin, says the devout Gerson, is that of Mother of God, all the more because that character gives her authority and natural dominion over the Lord of the whole world: *Quoniam per hoc habet veluti auctoritatem, et naturale dominium ad totius mundi Dominum.*[2] One must not

[1] Luke 2, 51.
[2] *Serm. de Annunt.*

10

imagine that her Son, having given her this power on earth, would take it away from her now that she is reigning in heaven. His respect and love for her now are just as great as when He was on earth.

It is only right, therefore, to believe that she is as powerful in heaven as she was on earth and that she still maintains there a measure of authority over her Divine Son. *Eadem potestas est Matris et Filii,* says Arnold of Chartres; or as Richard of St. Lawrence puts it: *Quae ab omnipotente Filio omnipotens facta est.* The Son and the Mother, having but one and the same flesh, but one and the same heart and will, have also, in a certain way, but one and the same power.

Let us listen to the words of a worthy and learned prelate, George, Archbishop of Nicomedia. Addressing the glorious Virgin he says: "Nothing resists thy might, everything obeys thy imperium; He who is born of thee hath raised thee above all things; thy Creator makes thy glory His and deems Himself honored by those who honor thee; thy Son rejoices beholding the honor that we give thee, and as if He were paying off the obligations He hath to thee, He gladly grants thee whatsoever thou dost ask Him: *Nihil, O Virgo, tuae resistit potentiae; tuam gloriam Filius putat esse propriam, et quasi exsolvens debitum, implet petitiones tuas."* [3]

We know for certain, says St. Anselm, that the Blessed Virgin is so filled with grace and merit that she always obtains the fruition of her desires: *Scimus beatam Virginem tanti esse meriti et gratiae apud Deum, ut nihil eorum, quae velit efficere, possit aliquatenus effectu carere.* [4] It is impossible, says St. Germanus, Archbishop of Constantinople, that her prayers should not be heard, everywhere and in all things, because her Divine Son is always submissive to her behests: *Non potest non exaudiri, cum Deus ut verae Matris suae, quoad omnia, et per omnia, et in omnibus morem gerat.* [5]

Utrinque stupor, says St. Bernard, *utrinque miraculum;* miracles on both sides. *Quod Deus feminae obtemperet, humilitas absque exemplo; et quod Deo femina principetur, sublimitas sine socio:* "That God

[3] *Orat. de Oblat. Deiparae.*
[4] *De Excel. Virg.,* cap. 12.
[5] *Serm. 2 in B. Mar. dormit.*

should obey a woman is humility unexampled, and that a woman should command God is an authority which has no like." Hence it is that St. Peter Damian is not afraid to say that our Blessed Lady appears in heaven, before the sacred altar of our reconciliation, *non solum rogans sed imperans,* "not only as a servant but as a mother who commands." [6] *Roga Patrem, jube nato, jure Matris impera,* sings the Church of Paris in one of its sequences: "When thou hast aught to ask of the Eternal Father, O holy Virgin, resort to prayer and supplication; but when it is a question of the Son, then thy maternal authority gives thee the right to utter a command."

If anyone should claim that here the creature is being put above the Creator, I would ask him whether Sacred Scripture raises Josue above God when it says that the sun stood still and God obeyed the voice of a man. [7] No, this is not putting the creature above the Creator; the fact is that the Son of God has such love and respect for His holy Mother that her prayer to Him is equal to a command.

The Blessed Virgin, says St. Albertus Magnus, [8] is able to entreat her Son for the salvation of her servants, and she is able to command Him with the authority of a Mother. This is the favor we ask of her, he adds, when we use the words: *Monstra te esse Matrem.* It is a frequent prayer of the Church, a prayer that is most pleasing to her and most profitable to our souls. It is as if we said to her: Most holy Mother of God, let us see the incomparable mercies with which thy motherly heart is filled on behalf of thy most unworthy children; show us the mighty power that thy most benign heart hath upon the most merciful Heart of thy beloved Son: *Monstra te esse Matrem, sumat per te preces, qui pro nobis natus tulit esse tuus.*

[6] *Serm. 1 de Nativ. B. Mariae.*
[7] Josue 10, 14.
[8] *De Laud. Virg.,* lib. 2.

CHAPTER 4

THE SACRED HEART OF JESUS WAS FILLED WITH BITTER SORROW AT THE SIGHT OF HIS LOVING MOTHER'S ANGUISH DURING HIS PASSION

As THE ADORABLE HEART of our Saviour was on fire with infinite love for His most holy Mother, the anguish which He bore in seeing her plunged into a sea of sorrow at the time of His Passion was beyond the power of human word or thought. The Blessed Virgin was the Mother of our Redeemer and she ever sustained in her heart an unceasing combat of love. She knew that it was God's will that her Beloved Son should suffer and die to save souls. Thus her most ardent love for that divine will and for the salvation of souls placed her in utter submission to the commands of God. Her incomparable motherly love for her dear Son, however, caused her unspeakable sorrow, in view of the torments that He was to suffer to redeem the world.

The saints teach that, when the day of His Passion had come, in accordance with the loving obedience with which He always honored His holy Mother, and the goodness He always showed in consoling His friends in their affliction, He took leave of His dear Mother before the beginnings of His sufferings. To do all things out of obedience to the will of His Father and His Mother, since she had not a will different from the Father's, He asked permission of her to carry out what His Eternal Father had commanded Him. He told her that it was the will of the Father that she should accompany Him to the foot of the Cross and that, after His death, she should wrap His body in a shroud and place it in the tomb. The saints also teach that He commanded her what to do and where to remain until His resurrection.

It is also possible that He revealed to her what He had to suffer, as much to prepare her as to encourage her to accompany Him in His sufferings. Because their interior sorrows were unutterable, they did not declare them to each other in words; their eyes met and their Hearts understood their mutual afflictions. The most perfect love of both and their entire conformity to the divine will did not permit any imperfection in their natural feelings. On the one hand, the Saviour being the Only Son of His beloved Mother felt very keenly her sorrows; but, on the other, being her God and willing to fortify her in the greatest sorrow ever borne by a human being, He consoled her by His divine words, which she heard and kept carefully in her Heart. He poured an abundance of new grace into her soul so that she might endure and overcome the exceedingly terrible sorrows prepared for her. These sorrows were so great that if it had been possible and fitting for her to suffer in place of her Son, it would have been easier for her to do so. Her torments would thus have been much more bearable than the sight of her Son's Passion. It would have been infinitely preferable for her to give her life for Him than to watch Him suffer such dreadful tortures. Since God had willed otherwise, she offered her Heart and Jesus gave His body, so that each should suffer what God had ordained. Mary had to suffer all the torments of her Son in her extremely sensitive Heart; Jesus had to endure in His body inexplicable torments and in His Heart the inconceivable sufferings of His holy Mother.

When He had taken leave of His Mother, the Saviour plunged Himself into the immense ocean of His sorrows, and His desolate Mother accompanied Him in spirit as she remained in constant prayer. Thus that sad day began for her with prayers, tears, inner agonies, and a most perfect submission to the divine will, as she uttered in the depths of her Heart what her Son said to His Father in the Garden of Olives: "Father, not my will but thine be done." [1] The night that our Redeemer was seized in the Garden of Olives, the Jews led Him, bound and manacled, first to the House of Annas, then to that of Caiphas, where, weary of mocking and insulting Him, they kept Him a prisoner until the next day.

[1] Luke 22, 42.

St. John the Evangelist also left the house of Caiphas, whether by an order from our Saviour or by some divine inspiration, and went to the house of the Blessed Virgin to inform her of what had taken place. Who, O my God, could express the grief and sorrow of the Mother of Jesus as His beloved disciple recounted what had happened since the opening events of the Passion? Surely the feelings and the griefs of them both were such that whatever one might say of them would be as naught compared with the reality. They conversed more with their hearts than with their tongues, more with tears than with words, particularly the Blessed Virgin, whose grief was so intense that she could give no outward expression to it. Later, when the time came to accompany her Only Son to Calvary, she set out at daybreak in silence, even as her Divine Son, her Lamb, took up His Cross without a word. She bathed the way with her tears and her Heart set up a thousand ardent sighs to heaven. Let the devout followers of this sorrowing Virgin henceforth gladly pursue a way whereby they can accompany her in her sorrows.

The Jews led the Saviour to the house of Pilate and Herod, with every sort of insult and shame, but His sad Mother could not see Him because of the multitude and the noise of the people, until that moment when Pilate, after the scourging and the crowning of thorns, showed Him to the populace. Then it was that she heard the voices of the rabble, the uproar of the city, the insults vomited forth against Her Son, the outrages done Him, the blasphemies flung at Him. Her heart underwent immeasurable suffering and her eyes streamed with tears: *Deduc quasi torrentem lacrymas.*[2] As she had placed all her love in Him, she desired His presence above all else, even though it must have afflicted her the most, for love can be so ardent that it endures much less the absence of the object loved than the pain caused by the beloved's presence, however great the pain.

In all this bitterness and anguish, passing all imagination, this innocent Mother aspired to the sight of her Divine Son. Finally she saw Him all torn from head to foot with whips. His sacred head was pierced with cruel thorns, His adorable face bruised, swollen, stained with blood and spittle. With a rope around His neck and His hands

[2] Lam. 2, 18.

bound, He wore the scarlet robe of mockery. Well did He know that His sorrowful Mother was there; and she, too, knew full well that His divine majesty read the feelings of her Heart, which was pierced with sorrows not inferior to those He bore in his own body. There she heard the false testimony given against Him; she heard them prefer Barrabas, a thief and a murderer. She heard thousands of voices shouting in anger: *Tolle, tolle, crucifige, crucifige!* [3] She heard the cruel and unjust sentence pronounced against the Author of life. She saw upraised the Cross, on which they were to crucify Him; she saw Him bearing it on His shoulders and beginning His march to Calvary. She followed his blood-stained footsteps and washed the way with as many tears as He shed drops of blood; and she bore inwardly the burden of the Cross, as heavy upon her heart as upon His shoulders.

At last she reached Calvary, accompanied by the holy women who sought to console her. Like her gentle Lamb she was silent, suffering unspeakable agony, hearing the hammer-blows struck by the executioners on the nails fastening her Son to the Cross. As she was extremely weak from her night of watching, tears and fasting, when she saw Him whom she loved more deeply than herself raised on the Cross, without being able to relieve Him in any way, she fell into the arms of those accompanying her, as ordinarily happens under the stress of great and excessive sorrow. Then as her tears dried, she lay there, pale, trembling mightily. No other fragrant water could be found to throw upon her face but the tears of grief of those who were supporting her, until such time as her Son restored her strength that she might accompany Him unto death. [4]

Whereupon, shedding new streams of tears, she began to suffer a fresh martyrdom of sorrow at the sight of her Son and her God hanging upon the Cross. Nevertheless, this did not prevent her from performing, within her soul, the office of mediatrix between God and

[3] John 19, 15

[4] The fact mentioned here by St. John Eudes is reported by several authors, but the most reliable theologians reject it because they think it is in opposition to the perfect control of all the notions of sensibility which they unanimously recognize in Mary, and to the quasi-priestly role that she had to fulfil during the Passion of her divine Son. Cf. Terrien: *La Mère des hommes,* I, p. 200, note 5.

sinners, cooperating with their Redeemer in saving them, and offering to the Father for them His blood, His sufferings, and His death, with the most ardent desire for their eternal happiness. On the one hand, the unspeakable love that she bore her dear Child made her fear to behold Him expire and die; on the other, it filled her with sorrow that His torments were dragging on so long, only to end in His death. Although she wanted the Eternal Father to soften the rigor of His torments, she also wished to conform wholly to His every command. Thus divine love engendered in her Heart a combat between conflicting desires and feelings which, from this same love, caused her to suffer unspeakable sorrows.

These sacred Lambs, divine and human, beheld and understood each other and communicated to each other their sorrows. It may be said with certainty that no one can understand their anguish except the two Hearts of Son and Mother who, loving each other perfectly, together suffered these cruel torments. Their mutual love being the measure of their sorrows, those who consider their excruciating pain are all the less able to understand it the further they are from comprehending the love of such a Son for such a Mother, and of such a Mother for such a Son.

The sorrows of the Blessed Virgin went on increasing. They were being renewed continually by new insults and torments inflicted on her Son by the Jews in their wrath. What sorrow when she heard Him utter these words: "My God, my God, why hast Thou forsaken me?" [5] What sorrow to see gall and vinegar given Him to quench His burning thirst! What sorrow when she watched Him die on the gibbet between criminals! What sorrow to behold His Heart pierced with a lance! What sorrow when she received Him dead, taken down from the Cross and placed in her arms! What sorrow when the disciples took His holy body from her embrace to enclose it in the sepulchre! With what sorrow must she have returned home, there to await His resurrection! How gladly would the holy Virgin have suffered all the pains of her Son rather than witness His endurance!

It is a result which perfect charity produces in the hearts of those who strive to imitate their Divine Father and their good Mother that

[5] Matt. 27, 46.

they bear with joy their own afflictions and keenly feel those of others. Thus it is easier for them to endure pain themselves than to see the loved ones suffering. That is what our Saviour did throughout the course of His life and particularly on the day of His Passion. Knowing that the traitor had sold Him for money, He showed far deeper concern over the lost soul of Judas (saying it would have been better for him if he had never been born rather than merit damnation), than over the torments that He had to suffer by betrayal.

He also showed to the weeping women who were following Him as He carried His cross on His shoulders, how the tribulations which they and the city of Jerusalem would have to suffer, were more painful to Him than all that He was undergoing. "Daughters of Jerusalem," He said to them, "weep not over me; but weep for yourselves, and for your children. For behold, the days shall come wherein they will say: Blessed are the barren, and the wombs that have never borne, and the paps that have not given suck." [6]

Even while He was fastened to the cross, forgetting His own torments, He made it clear that the trials of sinners were felt more by Him than His own sufferings, in that He prayed His Father to pardon them. From this we know that His love for His creatures rendered Him more sensitive to their afflictions than to His own.

The greatest torture that our Saviour suffered on the Cross, a torture more painful to Him than His own bodily sufferings, was to see His most holy Mother whom He loved more than all creatures together, overwhelmed with sorrow. She was of all mothers the most perfect, the faithful companion of His journeys and of all His labors, who, being immaculate, deserved not to suffer for any fault that she had committed. Her motherly love was greater than that of all angels and saints. She saw Him suffering torments that never had nor ever will have their like. How great is the agony of such a Mother, who sees before her eyes such a Son so unjustly tortured and agonizing in a sea of sorrows, without being able to help Him! Truly this cross was so huge and heavy that no human soul is capable of comprehending it. It was a cross which was reserved for the grace, the love, and the heroic virtues of the Mother of God.

[6] Luke 23, 28-29.

The fact that she was the innocent Mother of God did not prevent her from suffering such great torture. On the contrary, her Son would not permit anyone, even those who were crucifying Him, to dare to offer her insult or cause her grief. Desiring to make her like unto Himself, whose love was the principal and first cause of His sufferings and His death, He also willed that His love for His Mother and her love for Him should be the cause of the martyrdom of His heart at the end of His life, just as at the beginning it had been the source of His joys and satisfaction.

The Son of God witnessed from His cross all the griefs and sorrows of the holy Heart of His Blessed Mother; He heard her sighs, He saw her tears and the loneliness in which she was to remain after His death. Each vision was a new torment and a new martyrdom for the divine Heart of Jesus. Thus everything was present that could afflict and crucify the most lovable Hearts of the Son and the Mother. Therefore, some authorities think that when the Saviour spoke from the Cross to His sorrowful Mother, He did not wish to call her Mother, so as not to cause her more pain. He spoke only words which showed that He had not forgotten her and that, in accordance with His Father's will, He was succoring her in her loneliness, giving her the beloved disciple to be her son, saying: *Mulier, ecce filius tuus*— "Woman, behold thy son;" and to the disciple, "Behold thy Mother," *Ecce Mater tua*.[7] Henceforth, St. John remained bound to the service of the Queen of heaven, honoring her as his Mother and serving her as his Lady, esteeming the service to her as the greatest favor that he could receive in this world from his loving Master.

All sinners have a share in this grace of St. John, for he represented all human beings at the foot of the Cross and our Saviour beheld them all in him; so in speaking to him He was addressing all men in general and each soul in particular, saying, *Ecce Mater tua*—"Behold thy Mother." I give you my Mother to be yours, and I give you to her as her children. What a precious gift! What an inestimable treasure! What an incomparable grace! What an obligation we have to our Saviour in His unspeakable goodness! What thanks we should render Him! He has given His Divine Father to be our Father; and

[7] John 19, 26-27.

He gives us His most holy Mother to be our Mother, so that we shall have with Him but one and the same Father and Mother. We are not worthy to be the slaves of this great Queen, and lo! He makes us her children! What reverence and humility we must have for such a Mother! What zeal and affection in her service! What pains we must take to imitate her holy virtues, so that there will be some resemblance between Mother and children!

This gentle Mother received great consolation when she heard the voice of her Dear Son. At the hour of death any word whatsoever from one's child or dear friend lends great comfort and peculiar consolation. Since those two Sacred Hearts, the Hearts of such a Son and of such a Mother so well understood each other, the Blessed Virgin accepted most readily St. John as her son, and in him all sinners in general, knowing well that that was the intention of her dying Son. He was shedding His blood for sinners, and their sins were the cause of His death. He desired in that last hour to remove from them any possible mistrust of Him, when they saw the great sufferings that they had caused Him by their sins. To that end He gave them His most valued treasure, a treasure most capable of influencing Him, His most holy Mother, so that by her mediation and protection they might have the confident assurance of being received and welcomed by His divine majesty. One cannot doubt, therefore, the inestimable love of the Mother of goodness for sinners, since, in that spiritual begetting at the foot of the Cross, she suffered unspeakable pain which was absent from the virgin birth of her Son and her God.

All these things clearly show that the sorrows of the Mother and the sufferings of the Son culminate in immense graces, blessings, and favors for sinners. What an obligation we have, therefore, to honor, to love and to praise those two most lovable Hearts of Jesus and Mary; to employ our whole life in serving and glorifying them; and to endeavor to imprint on our hearts a perfect image of their most eminent virtues! It is impossible to please them if we follow any other path except the one they trod upon earth.

CHAPTER 5

THE SACRED HEART OF JESUS IS A FURNACE OF LOVE FOR THE CHURCH TRIUMPHANT, MILITANT AND SUFFERING

IT IS CERTAINLY TRUE that this adorable Heart is a burning furnace of divine love, radiating its fire and flame in all directions, in heaven, on earth, and even in hell: in heaven in the Church Triumphant, on earth in the Church Militant, and in purgatory in the Church Suffering, and to some degree even in the hell of the damned.

If we lift our eyes and hearts to heaven, to the Church Triumphant, what shall we see? We shall behold an innumerable army of saints, patriarchs, prophets, apostles, martyrs, confessors and virgins. What are all these saints? They are so many flames from the immense furnace of the divine Heart of Jesus. Is it not the love of that kind Heart which brought them into the world, enlightened them with the light of faith, and gave them strength to conquer the devil, the world and the flesh? Is it not the goodness of that amiable Heart which adorned them with all virtues, sanctified them in this world and glorified them in the other; which kindled in their hearts the love they bear to God, inspired their lips with His divine praises, which is the source of all that is great and holy and admirable in them? If then one celebrates during the course of the year so many feasts in honor of these same saints, what a solemnity is due to this divine Heart which is the principle of everything that is glorious and noble in all the saints!

Let us come down to earth and see what is most worthy and great in the Church Militant. It is the holy Sacraments—the Sacrament of Baptism by which we are made children of God; Confirmation, which gives us the Holy Spirit; Penance, which washes away our sins and restores us to God's favor; the Blessed Eucharist, which feeds our souls with the flesh and blood of the Son of God, making us live by His life; Matrimony, which forms children for God, to serve and honor Him on earth and to love and praise Him forever in heaven; Holy Orders, which gives to the Church priests who shall continue the functions of the great High Priest and thus cooperate with Him in the great work of the salvation of the world, so that they bear the name and the character of saviours in Holy Scripture: *Ascendent salvatores in montem Sion;* [1] and Extreme Unction, which at our departure from this world fortifies us against the enemies of our salvation, who at that last hour make their final endeavor to ruin us.

The seven Sacraments are so many inexhaustible fountains of grace and holiness, which have their source in the immense ocean of the Sacred Heart of our Saviour; they are so many flames of a divine furnace from which proceed all spiritual blessings. But the brightest of those flames is the most Holy Eucharist. It is true that this great Sacrament is a compendium of all the wonders of the power, wisdom and goodness of God, but it is also true that it is one of the fruits of the incomparable Heart of Jesus and one of the flames of that wondrous furnace.

Since a solemn feast is celebrated by Holy Church in honor of the Blessed Sacrament, what a solemnity should also be kept in honor of His most Sacred Heart, which is the source of all that is great and rare and precious in this august Sacrament?

Let us, as it were, descend in spirit to purgatory, to the Church Suffering. What is purgatory? It is the awe-inspiring throne of divine justice, which metes out in this place punishments so terrible that St. Thomas says: *Minima poena purgatorii excedit omnes poenas hujus mundi.* "The slightest pain suffered there surpasses all the sufferings of this world." [2] St. Augustine says the same thing as the Angelic Doctor. [3] Nevertheless, the terrible justice of God does not hold such

---

[1] Abd. 1, 21.

[2] *Summa* 111ª, q. 46, a. 6, ad 3.

[3] "Gravior est ille ignis, quam quidquid potest homo pati in hac vita." *Super Psalm.* 37. "Ille purgatorius ignis durior erit, quam quidquid potest in hoc saeculo poenarum videri, aut cogitari, aut sentiri." *Serm. 4 pro defunctis.*

sway in purgatory that mercy has no part there. Mercy with justice has constituted purgatory, to open paradise, which would remain closed to the majority of men if purgatory did not exist, because it is a truth of our faith that nothing contaminated shall enter heaven: *Nihil coinquinatum intrabit in regnum caelorum.* [4] Thus a soul, even though it had but one venial sin on quitting the body, would never enter paradise unless the merciful Saviour had established purgatory to purify it. And so purgatory is a result of the goodness and charity of the most benign Heart of our Redeemer.

Let us descend still lower. Let us go in spirit into hell, since St. Chrysostom declares that not one of those who thus go there during this life to inspire themselves to the work of their salvation with fear and trembling shall descend there after death.

What is hell? It is a place of torment, according to the Holy Gospel: *Locus tormentorum;* [5] it is *gehenna ignis;* [6] *supplicium aeternum;* [7] "the pain of fire, an eternal punishment"; in short, it is the place of the vengeance and anger of God. But the infinite mercy of the Sacred Heart of Jesus is manifested there in three ways.

First, His goodness provides that the damned are not punished as much as they deserve; for sin deserves infinite punishment, seeing that it is an offense committed against a God who infinitely deserves to be served and obeyed, and against a God to whom we have infinite obligations. Sin deserves infinite punishment not only as to extent and duration, but also intensively as to the degree and quality of the punishment. Now, although the pains of the reprobate are infinite as to extent and duration, they are limited as to intensiveness and degree, seeing that Our Lord could increase them ever more and more. This He does not do because of the ineffable goodness of His most tender Heart.

Secondly, His justice has established a hell to punish the wicked who die in their sins, but His mercy too has fashioned it, says St. Chrysostom, to inspire the fear of God in the hearts of the good and

[4] Apoc. 21, 27.
[5] Luke 16, 28.
[6] Matt. 18, 9.
[7] Matt. 25, 46.

to lead them to work out their salvation *cum timore et tremore*,[8] with fear and trembling.

Thirdly, the unparalleled goodness of our Saviour employs the fires of hell to enkindle in our hearts the fire of divine love. In what way? In this manner. If you had deserved punishment by fire, what an obligation you would have to love the person who delivered you from such a heavy penalty! How few persons there are on earth who have never committed a mortal sin! There are very few indeed. And what was the just desert of all those who offended God mortally even but once in their whole life? They have merited hell, but on them alone does it depend to be freed therefrom. To whom do they owe this obligation? To the immense charity of the most kind Heart of our Redeemer, which gives them infinite obligations to serve and to love Him. Acknowledge that the loving kindnesses of the amiable Heart of this divine Saviour are exceedingly admirable; that He uses even the fires of hell to draw us to love Him and hence to belong to the number of those who shall possess Him eternally.

And so this divine furnace, the adorable Heart of Jesus, diffuses everywhere its fiery flames, in heaven, on earth, and even in hell. O ineffable goodness! O wondrous love! O God of my heart, would that I possessed all the hearts that have ever been, are, and shall be, in heaven, on earth, and under the earth, to employ them in loving, praising and glorifying Thee unceasingly! O Jesus, only Son of God, only Son of Mary, I offer Thee the most loving Heart of Thy divine Mother which is more precious and pleasing to Thee than all hearts. O Mary, Mother of Jesus, I offer Thee the most adorable Heart of Thy Well-beloved Son, who is the life and love and joy of thy Heart.

[8] Eph. 6, 5.

CHAPTER 6

THE SACRED HEART OF JESUS IS A FURNACE OF LOVE FOR EACH ONE OF US

To APPRECIATE this truth, let us consider the wondrous effects of the inconceivable goodness and the unspeakable love of the Sacred Heart towards us. Two of these effects which embody many more are here given.

The first is that of having delivered us from the abyss of evils into which sin had plunged us. By sin we were made enemies of God, the object of His wrath and curse, excommunicated from the Most Holy Trinity, anathematized by the Father, the Son and the Holy Ghost, separated from the company of angels, banished from the home of our Heavenly Father; by sin we were driven from paradise, cast into hell, plunged into the devouring flames of eternal fire, subjected to the terrible tyranny of Satan, enslaved by demons, given over to their rage and fury, condemned to the rightful punishments of hell, all without hope of succor or relief.

Exceedingly terrible as are those evils there is yet one which exceeds them all. What is that but sin, which is the evil of evil and the sole cause of all the others on earth and in hell. What an evil is sin! To understand something of its malice, imagine all men who have lived, are now living, and will live upon earth; imagine that each of them possesses the holiness of a St. John the Baptist; imagine also all the angels of heaven as having taken mortal flesh and being joined to the multitude of men. Even if all these men and angels were to shed their blood to the last drop and suffer all the torments of hell for eternity, they would not be able to deliver us from the tiniest venial sin; they would not be able to render perfect and worthy satisfaction

25

to God for the offense done Him, nor consequently to free us from the slightest evil we should have merited by that sin, nor give us that drop of water which the rich man craved so long ago.

If one venial sin is so great an evil, what of mortal sin? What is it to be the slave of that infernal monster, which is more hideous and terrible than all the monsters and dragons of earth and hell?

Such is the pit of evils into which we had been plunged, from which there was no hope of escape, since all human powers and all the forces of heaven and earth were powerless to deliver us. Yet it has transpired, by a boon which we cannot comprehend, that we were liberated! To whom do we owe this? To the most loving Heart of our adorable Redeemer. We were delivered from so many evils by the immeasurable goodness, the infinite mercy, and the matchless love of that divine Heart. What had we done, what service rendered, to constrain Him thereto? Nothing whatever. It was out of purest love that He honored us with such a favor. What did He do to obtain for us so great a blessing? He did and suffered all. The cost to Him was dear, His blood, His life, a thousand torments, and a most cruel and shameful death. What obligations we have to honor, praise, and love that most benign Heart in return for all these benefits!

Suppose a man is a bandit-gunman. He has robbed a wealthy merchant by violence. He is caught, imprisoned, tried, condemned to death, and there he is in the hands of the hangman who is putting the rope around his neck. The merchant arrives at that very moment. By dint of money, the entreaties of friends, and even by the offer of his own life for the culprit, he obtains a pardon for the criminal and sets him free. How great is the bandit's debt to his rescuer!

For our crimes we were condemned to the pains of hell. The only-begotten Son of God, out of the inconceivably abundant goodness of His divine Heart, suffered a most atrocious and shameful death in order to deliver us. Try to estimate how indebted we are to that adorable Heart. An elephant will give itself entirely for the rest of its life to serve a man who had released it from a pit. What shall I give in return to Thee, my Saviour, and what shall I do for Thy love of me? Thou hast snatched me out of the frightful jaws of hell as often as ever I have fallen into them by sinning, or would have fallen if the charity of Thy dear Heart had not held me back. Does it take a dumb animal to teach me the lesson of gratitude which I owe Thee for Thy unspeakable mercies?

Such is the first effect, or rather the effect without number or measure of the tremendous love which the Sacred Heart of our Redeemer has manifested in delivering us from immeasurable evils. But it is not enough for him to have freed us from all those punishments; He would likewise shower us with inconceivable gifts. What a favor and fortune it is, not only to be snatched from hell but to be raised to heaven, to be made a citizen of paradise where there is a general exemption from all sorts of evils and where one possesses fully, entirely, unchangeably, eternally all sorts of boons! What a favor and a fortune to be associated with the angels, to be their companion, to be seated beside their throne, to live the angelic life, to be clothed with their glory, to enjoy their felicity, in short, to resemble the angels: *Erunt aequales angelis Dei!* [1]

What extraordinary fortune to be ranked with the children of God, the heirs of the great God, the co-heirs of the Son of God: *Videte qualem caritatem dedit nobis Pater, ut filii Dei nominemur et simus!* [2] What a remarkable privilege to be kings of an everlasting kingdom and to possess the same kingdom that the Father of Jesus has given to His Son: *Sicut disposuit mihi Pater, et ego dispono vobis regnum!* [3] What a blessed invitation to eat at the table of the King of heaven: *Ut edatis et bibatis super mensam meam.* [4] What a great joy to be clothed in the glorious royal robe of the King of kings: *Caritatem quam dedisti mihi, dedi eis!* [5] What a supreme favor to share the throne of the Sovereign Monarch of the universe: *Qui vicerit, dabo ei sedere mecum in throno meo!* [6] What an incomparable blessing to dwell quietly with our Saviour in the bosom and in the adorable Heart of His Divine Father: *Pater, quos dedisti mihi,*

[1] Luke 20, 36.
[2] John 3, 1.
[3] Luke 22, 29.
[4] *Ibid.* 30.
[5] John 17, 22.
[6] Apoc. 3, 21.

*volo ut ubi sum ego, et illi sint mecum.*⁷ "Father, I will that where
I am, they also whom thou hast given me may be with me." Where
art Thou, my Saviour? *In sinu Patris,* "in the bosom of the Father,"
says St. John. ⁸

What a fortune, moreover, to share all the good things that God
possesses! He who has God shall enjoy all the manifold glory, happiness and wealth of God: *Amen dico vobis, super omnia bona sua
constituet eum.* ⁹ What a blessing to be wholly transformed into God,
to be clothed, filled, penetrated with all the perfections of God, more
perfectly than the iron in the midst of the furnace is penetrated by the
qualities of the fire! Finally, what a blessing to be united to God:
*Sicut tu Pater in me, et ego in te, ita et ipsi in nobis unum sunt:
divinae consortes naturae.* ¹⁰ What a privilege to be by grace and by
participation what God is by nature and by essence!

What created mind can understand these surpassing gifts? Could
all the tongues of men and angels express the least part of them? Is
it not true what St. Paul says, that all those blessings are so great that
"eye hath not seen, nor ear heard, neither hath it entered into the
heart of man, what things God hath prepared for them that love
him:" *Nec oculus vidit nec auris audivit, nec in cor hominis ascendit
quae praeparavit Deus diligentibus se.* ¹¹

Now, to whom do we owe all those blessings? To the boundless
generosity and infinite love of the most kind Heart of our lovable
Saviour. Hence, what honor, what praise, what thanksgiving we must
render Him, and with what devotion we must celebrate the solemnity
of that most august Heart! Suppose that the aforesaid merchant who
was robbed not only delivered the gunman from the hands of the
executioner and from the shameful death he was ready to suffer, but
also gave him half of his goods. How would that criminal ever be
able to repay such goodness?

Our divine Saviour has done more for us. Not only has He delivered us from eternal death and all the tortures accompanying it,

⁷ John 17, 24.
⁸ *Ibid.* 1, 18.
⁹ Matt. 24, 47.
¹⁰ John 17, 21.
¹¹ I Cor. 2, 9.

but He has also heaped upon us a superabundance of unspeakable blessings. Indeed, He has given us all His blessings without reserve.

What shall we give Him in return? *Quid retribuam Domino, pro omnibus quae retribuit mihi?* [12] If we had the hearts of as many Seraphim as there are stars in the sky, atoms in the air, blades of grass on the earth, grains of sand and drops of water in the sea, and if we devoted them solely to love and glorify Him, it would be as nothing compared with the love He has for us and the obligations we have of consecrating our hearts to Him.

Yet what are we and the great majority of men doing? Is it not true that we treat this adorable Redeemer as ungratefully as if we had never received any boon from Him? Is it not true that we treat Him as if He had done us all the evil in the world? But is it not true that He has neglected nothing, that if it came even to all His glory and His own safety, He would not have been able to do more than He has done for love of us? *Quid potui facere et non feci?* [13] If it were possible, He says to St. Bridget, that I should suffer all the torments of My Passion as many times as there are souls in hell, I would most gladly suffer them, for charity is as much aflame in my Heart now as it was then.

Even so, is it not still true that the majority of men on earth treat that loving Saviour as if He were their enemy? What insults, what crimes, what cruelty and abuse could they practise against Him that they do not already practise? In short, what more despicable thing could they do than to crucify Him every day? Yes, crucify Him; for anyone who mortally offends Him crucifies Him, *rursus Christum crucifigentes,*[14] and commits a greater crime than did the Jews, for they did not know Him.

Let us detest and recoil from such ingratitude and such abominable wickedness. Let us open our ears to the voice, or rather the voices of our Saviour. I say "voices," for all the evils from which He has delivered us and all the blessings without number that He has given

[12] Ps. 115, 12.
[13] Isa. 5, 4.
[14] Heb. 6, 6.

us are so many voices crying out to us: *Sic Deus dilexit nos.*[15] "God so loved us." Therefore let us love Him who so loves us. If a man of no account, the weakest and lowest of all men, should manifest some kindliness towards us, we could not help loving him. Nay, if even a dumb animal, a mongrel, for instance, attaches itself to us and does us some slight service, we love it. Why then should we not love God who is our creator, our preserver, our ruler, our king, our most faithful friend, our most loving father, our treasure, our glory, our supreme good, our life, our heart, our all? He is all heart and soul and love for us.

"O my Saviour, I know not if I have yet begun to love Thee as I ought. *Dixi, nunc coepi.*[16] I now mean to love Thee with all my heart with all my soul, and with all my strength. I renounce forever all that is contrary to Thy holy love. Let me die a thousand deaths rather than ever offend Thee. I give Thee my heart; take full and absolute possession of it; destroy in it everything not pleasing to Thee, and rather destroy it itself than to allow it not to love Thee: *aut amare Jesum meum, aut mori.* But am I giving Thee anything in giving Thee my empty heart? O my Lord, if I had the hearts of as many Seraphim as Thy omnipotence could create, with what joy would I consecrate them all to Thee! I offer Thee the precious heart of Thy most worthy Mother, who has more love for Thee than all hearts that have been, are, or shall be. O Mother of Jesus, love Thy Adorable Son for me. O good Jesus, love Thy sweet Mother for me. O all ye citizens of the heavenly Jerusalem, love Jesus and Mary for me, and unite me with your great love, now and eternally."

[15] John 4, 11.
[16] Ps. 76, 11.

CHAPTER 7

THE SACRED HEART OF JESUS IS A FURNACE OF LOVE FOR US IN THE BLESSED SACRAMENT

St. Bernard appropriately refers to the Blessed Sacrament of the Eucharist as "the Love of loves," *Amor amorum.* If we use the eyes of faith to contemplate the marvelous effects of our Saviour's ineffable goodness to us in this adorable mystery, we shall see eight flames of love issuing continually from this wondrous furnace.

The first flame is the inconceivable love of the Sacred Heart of Jesus which impelled Him to imprison Himself in this Sacrament and has constrained Him to abide there continuously night and day, for nearly two thousand years, to be always with us, so as to fulfil the promise of these words: *Ecce ego vobiscum sum onmibus diebus, usque ad consummationem saeculi.* "Behold I am with you all days, even to the consummation of the world." [1] He is the Good Shepherd who wishes always to be with His flock. He is the divine Physician who wishes always to be at the bedside of His patients. He is the Father full of affection who never leaves His children. He is the Friend most loyal and tender, whose delight it to be with His friends: *Deliciae meae esse cum filiis hominum.* [2]

The second flame of this fiery furnace is the love of our Saviour's adorable Heart vibrating in great and significant actions on our behalf in this Sacrament. He is there adoring, praising and glorifying His Father unceasingly for us, to satisfy to the full our infinite obligations of adoring, praising and glorifying. He is there continu-

[1] Matt. 28, 20.
[2] Prov. 8, 31.

ally giving thanks to the Father for all the corporal and spiritual blessings, natural and supernatural, temporal and eternal, which He has ever given to us, which He gives at each moment, and plans to give us, provided we interpose no obstacle. He is there loving His Father for us, paying to the full our debts and obligations of loving Him. He is there offering His merits to satisfy His Father's justice and to pay Him on our behalf what we owe Him by reason of our sins. He is there continually praying to His Father for all our spiritual and temporal needs. *Semper vivens ad interpellandum pro nobis.*[3]

The third flame of this furnace is the infinite love of our dear Redeemer, who exercises His omnipotence so as to perform in this adorable Sacrament many stupendous miracles, changing bread into His body and wine into His blood, and performing several other wonders incomparably surpassing all those of Moses, of the prophets, and of the apostles, and even of our Saviour during His sojourn on earth. All those miracles were performed only in Judea, while these take place throughout the universe. The visible miracles were transitory and of short duration; the invisible have been continuous for more than nineteen hundred years and they will endure till the end of time. The former were effected on bodies separated from their souls and then restored to life, on sick persons who were healed, on water changed to wine, but the latter are effected on the adorable body of God, on His Precious Blood, and even on the glory and grandeur of His divinity, which is hidden in this Sacrament.

The fourth flame is indicated in the inspired words of St. Peter, the Prince of the Apostles: *Misit Deus Filium suum benedicentem vobis.* "God hath sent his Son to bless you."[4] This Adorable Son has come filled with love for you and with a most ardent desire to pour out His blessings upon those who honor Him and love Him as their Father. It is chiefly in this divine Sacrament that He showers His blessings upon those who open the way to His grace.

The fifth flame is His immense love which constrains Him to give to us all the treasures of grace and holiness which He acquired

[3] Heb. 7, 25.
[4] Acts 3, 26.

on earth. To us He does give them, indeed, in the Blessed Eucharist, boons immeasurable and infinite, graces most abundant and special, provided we have the dispositions required for receiving them.

The sixth flame is that burning love always impelling Him to enrich us with the gifts and graces which He acquired by His Precious Blood, and to give Himself to us without reserve in Holy Communion. He gives us His divinity, His humanity, His divine person, His adorable body, His Precious Blood, His holy soul, in short, all that He has and all that He is, as God and as man. Consequently, He will give us His Eternal Father and His Holy Spirit which are inseparable from Him, just as He will inspire us with devotion to His most holy Mother, who everywhere follows her divine Lamb, much more than do the holy virgins of whom it is said: *Sequuntur Agnum quocumque ierit.*[5]

The seventh flame is the incredible love of the Blessed Saviour in immolating Himself continually for us, a love that surpasses in every way the charity by which He was immolated on the altar of the Cross. There He sacrificed Himself on Calvary only; here He sacrifices Himself all over the world by means of the Blessed Eucharist. There He immolated Himself once only; here He sacrifices Himself thousands of times daily. It is true that the Sacrifice of the Cross was accomplished in a sea of sorrows and that it is accomplished here in an ocean of joy and felicity, but the Heart of our Redeemer is still, in our day, as flaming with love for us as it was then. Jesus is ready, if it were possible and necessary for our salvation, to undergo the same sufferings that He bore in His immolation on Calvary, as many times as He sacrifices Himself on the altars throughout the world because of His infinite love for us.

The eighth flame of this wonderful furnace of love consists of the love that our most benign Redeemer manifests to us when He gives men continual evidence of His goodness at a time when He receives from them nothing but the most furious hatred imaginable. At what moment does He thus manifest such love? At the time of the institution of this divine Sacrament, the last day of His life, the night before His death. At that very moment men are not less

---

[5] Apoc. 14, 4.

moved with rage and fury against Him than the devils themselves; for what does He say? *Haec est hora vestra, et potestas tenebrarum.*[6]

"O my Saviour, on that first Holy Thursday evening, Thy thoughts were only of peace, charity, and good will for men, whereas the Jews thought only of malice and cruelty. Thou didst seek only to save them; they sought only to do away with Thee. Thy whole Heart and Thy whole mind were bent on breaking the chains that held them bound as the slaves of demons; and they would sell Thee, betray Thee and deliver Thee into the hands of Thy cruel enemies. Thou wast preoccupied with establishing an adorable Sacrament whereby always to abide with them, but they were striving to drive Thee from the world, to banish Thee from off the earth, and even to destroy Thee if they could but do so. Thou didst prepare for them on earth boundless graces and in heaven thrones magnificent and glorious crowns, if they were willing to render themselves worthy of them, but they were preparing for Thee ropes, lashes, thorns, nails, lances, crosses, spittle, revilings, blasphemies and all sorts of shameful outrageous cruelties. Thou didst set before them a most delectable feast of Thy own flesh and blood, and they gave Thee gall and vinegar to drink. Thou didst give them Thy holy and immaculate body and they bruised it by blows, they cut it with their lashes, they pierced it in a thousand places with thorns and nails, they covered it with wounds from head to foot, they dismembered it on the Cross, causing it to suffer the most atrocious tortures. Finally, my Saviour, Thou didst love them more than Thy own life and blood since Thou didst sacrifice them for Thy enemies. In return, they rent Thy soul from Thy body by violence.

"What goodness! what charity! what love flowing from Thy adorable Heart, O my Saviour! What ingratitude! what wickedness! what cruelty stemming from the heart of man!

"What happened then still happens today. Thy most loving Heart, O Jesus, dwells in this Sacrament, burning with love for us. It is there continually performing thousands of good deeds towards us. How do we repay Thee, O Lord? We repay Thee with ingratitude and injuries a thousandfold, in thought, word and deed, trampling

[6] Luke 22, 53.

under foot Thy divine commandments and those of the Church. Ungrateful wretches, our most gracious Saviour so loved us that, while He was on earth, He would have died a thousand deaths for love of us if He had not miraculously preserved His life. He is still ready to die a hundred thousand times for us if it were possible and necessary for our salvation. Let us then die, die of sorrow in beholding our sins; let us die of shame that we have so little love for Him; let us die a thousand deaths rather than ever offend Him again. O my Saviour, grant us this favor, we implore Thee! O Mother of Jesus, obtain for us this grace from thy Well-beloved Son!"

CHAPTER 8

THE SACRED HEART OF JESUS IS A FURNACE BURNING WITH LOVE FOR US IN HIS SACRED PASSION

THE ENTIRE EARTHLY LIFE of our adorable Saviour was a continual exercise of charity and goodness towards us. But it was at the time of His Passion that He gave us the most remarkable proofs of His love. Then it was that out of the abundance of his charity, He suffered frightful torments to deliver us from the terrible punishments of hell and to win for us the everlasting joys of heaven. It was then that His adorable body was covered with wounds and bathed in His blood. His sacred head was pierced with sharp thorns, His hands and feet were transfixed with huge nails, His ears filled with blasphemies and curses, His lips moistened with gall and vinegar, and his soul forcibly and painfully wrenched from His body by the cruel Jews. At that time particularly His divine Heart was rent by countless painful, bleeding wounds. Indeed, one can count the wounds in the adorable Heart of Jesus. There are two kinds of wounds, resulting from two different causes.

The first cause of those most painful wounds in the Sacred Heart of our Redeemer is our sins. We read in the life of St. Catherine of Genoa that one day God let her see the horror of one tiny venial sin. She assures us that, although this vision lasted but a moment, she saw nevertheless an object so frightening that the blood froze in her veins and she swooned away in an agony that would have killed her if God had not preserved her to relate to others what she had seen. Wherefore she declared that if she were in the very depths of a sea of flaming fire and it were in her power to be set free, on condition that she should once more behold such a spectacle, she would choose to remain rather than to escape. If the sight of the smallest venial sin brought this saint to such a pass, what must we think of the state to which our Saviour was reduced by seeing all the sins of the universe? He had them continually before His eyes, and His vision being infinitely more powerful than that of St. Catherine, He could behold infinitely more horror.

He saw the immeasurable insult and dishonor caused His Father by all sins; He saw the damnation of a countless number of souls resulting from those sins. As He had infinite love for His Father and His creatures, the sight of all those sins rent His Heart with countless wounds, such that if we were able to count all the sins of men, which are more numerous than the drops of water in the sea, we would then be able to count the wounds of the loving Heart of Jesus.

The second cause of His wounds is the infinite love of His Sacred Heart for all His children, and his constant vision of all the afflictions and sufferings that are to happen to them, especially all the torments that His holy martyrs are to suffer. When a mother watches her beloved child suffering, she feels the pain more keenly than the child. Our Saviour's love for us is so tremendous that if all the love of all parents were centered in a single heart, it would not represent even a spark of the love for us that burns in His Heart. Our pains and sorrows, ever present to His vision and seen most clearly and distinctly, were so many wounds bleeding in His paternal Heart: *Vere nostros ipse tulit, et aegrotationes nostras portavit.*[1] These wounds were so painful and deep that they would have caused His death a thousand times over, even immediately after His birth, if he had not miraculously preserved Himself, because during His whole earthly life His Sacred Heart was continually pierced by many mortal wounds of love.

Therefore we have the greatest obligations to honor the gracious Heart that sustained so many wounds for love of us. We have potent reasons to fear new sins, thus giving him occasion to lament over us: *Super dolorem vulnerum meorum.* "They have added to the

---

[1] Isai. 53, 4; Matt. 8, 17.

grief of my wounds." [2] We ought to fear lest we be of the number of those of whom St. Paul says that they crucify Him afresh: *Rursus Christum crucifigentes!* [3] With what affection should we embrace, and endure all our afflictions, out of love for Jesus, our Saviour, since He first bore them for love of us! Should they not be most sweet to us, since they have already passed through His most gentle and loving Heart? What a horror we should have of our sins that have caused so many wounds and such intense grief to the divine Heart of our Redeemer!

We read in the life of St. Francis Borgia, of the Society of Jesus, that one day the saint was speaking in front of a crucifix to a great sinner whom he was exhorting to be converted, but could not soften the hard sinful heart. Suddenly the crucifix, or rather the Crucified Saviour, out of His wondrous and abundant goodness, spoke to the sinner and urged him to follow the advice of His servant. At the same time there issued blood from all His wounds. This was a sign that our Blessed Saviour was ready once again to shed His blood and to die for his salvation if need be. But in spite of such miraculous goodness, as the wretched man still remained adamant, there issued a stream of blood from the wound at His side, which gushed over him and struck him dead on the spot. O God, what a fearful sight!

Let us learn from the foregoing example that it is not our Redeemer's fault if we are lost. There are hearts so hard that, even if Jesus Himself were to come down from heaven to preach to them and they were to see Him covered with wounds and bathed in His blood, they would still not be converted. O my God, let us not be one of them, but give us the grace to open our ears to the voice of all the sacred wounds of Thy body and Thy heart, which are so many mouths through which Thou dost call to us unceasingly: *Redite, praevaricatores, ad cor.* "Return, ye transgressors, to the heart," [4] which means to My heart that is all yours, since I have given it entirely to you. Return to that most loving Heart of your Father, which is full of love and mercy for you, which will receive you and

[2] Ps. 68, 27.
[3] Heb. 6, 6.
[4] Isa. 46, 8.

welcome you home, heaping upon you all blessings. But *redite,* return without delay, completely, with all your affections. Leave sin, renounce hell, flee from all occasions of wickedness and embrace the practice of all virtues. Blessed are they who yield to that voice; cursed they who close their ears and harden their hearts like that unfortunate man just mentioned. *Cor durum male habebit in novissimo:* "A hard heart shall fear evil at the last." [5] Evil shall be the lot of the hard heart; it shall perish everlastingly; it shall abide in wrath forever, and shall suffer inconceivable and incomprehensible tortures eternally.

O my Saviour, I give Thee my heart; preserve it from this evil. O Mother of mercy, I give thee also my loving heart; do thou give it to thy Son, begging Him to rank it with the holy hearts that shall love the Son and the Mother forever!

[5] Eccl. 3, 27.

CHAPTER 9

THE SACRED HEART OF JESUS IS ONE WITH THE HEART OF THE FATHER AND THE HOLY GHOST; THE ADORABLE HEART OF BLESSED TRINITY IS A FURNACE OF BURNING LOVE FOR US

CHRISTIAN FAITH TEACHES that there are three Persons in the adorable mystery of the Holy Trinity; three Persons who have but one and the same divinity, one and the same power, wisdom, goodness, one and the same mind, will, and even one and the same heart. Thence it is that our Saviour, as God, has but one and the same Heart with the Father and the Holy Ghost; and as man, His humanly divine and divinely human Heart is but one also with the Heart of the Father and the Holy Ghost, by a unity of mind, love and will. Therefore to adore the Sacred Heart of Jesus is to adore the Heart of the Father, of the Son and of the Holy Ghost; to adore a Heart that is a burning furnace of love towards us. Into that furnace we must plunge so as to burn there forever. Unhappy they who shall be cast into the terrible furnace of eternal fire which is prepared for the devil and his angels, but blessed are they who shall be thrown into the eternal fire of divine love which enkindles the adorable Heart of the Father, the Son and the Holy Ghost for our sake. That we may stir ourselves to plunge in wholeheartedly, let us picture what that fire and that love are.

If you desire to learn the exact nature of the love of the paternal Heart of the divine Father of Jesus, listen to St. Paul: *Proprio Filio non pepercit, sed pro nobis omnibus tradidit illum.* "He that spared not even his own Son, but delivered him up for us all." [1] The Father sent His Only-begotten Son into this world to testify to us His love in a wondrous way. Before sending the Redeemer He knew full well how we would treat Him. He knew that, as Jesus must be born on earth to raise men up to heaven, His divine Mother would seek shelter for His birth and would find no place to lay His infant head. *Non erat locus in diversorio*.[2] He knew that, as soon as He was born, men would seek to slay Him, and that He would be compelled to flee and hide away in a foreign country. He knew that when He began to teach and preach the word of His Father they would regard Him as a mad man, they would repeatedly take up rocks to stone Him, and would lead Him into a high mountain to attempt to dash Him to destruction. He foresaw that they would bind and shackle Him like a thief, drag Him through the streets of Jerusalem like a criminal, subject Him to endless insults and torments and condemn Him to die the cruellest and most infamous death. After He had risen, they would endeavor to stifle any growing belief in His Resurrection. After He had established the Church and Sacraments to apply to souls the fruits of His Passion and death, even the majority of Christians would misuse these Sacraments, profane them and make them serve to their greater condemnation. Finally, He knew that in spite of His labor, sufferings, and death, too many souls would contemn His Precious Blood, making void and useless all that He accomplished for their salvation, because they would perish miserably.

"Thou seest all these things, O adorable Father, and yet Thou dost not hesitate to send us Thy Well-beloved Son. Who hath constrained Thee to do this? It is the utterly incomprehensible love of Thy fatherly Heart for us. O Father of mercies, it seems almost as if Thou dost love us more than Thyself and Thy Son (Thy Son being but one with Thee). Seemingly, for love of us, Thou hatest Thy Son, hence Thyself (Thou being but one with Him). O exceeding, inconceivable goodness! O wondrous love! There is something of that infinite love of the loving Heart of the Eternal Father for us."

[1] Rom. 8, 32.
[2] Luke 2, 7.

Would you now behold the incomprehensible love of the divine Heart of the Son of God? Hear Him speak: *Sicut dilexit me Pater, et ego dilexi vos.* "As the Father hath loved me, I also have loved you." [3] My Father so loves you that for love of you He hath surrendered me to death, the death of the Cross; and I so love you that for love of you I abandoned myself to the powers of darkness and to the wrath of my mortal enemies, the Jews: *Haec est hora vestra et potestas tenebrarum.* [4] O my Saviour, well may I say to Thee, with Thy faithful servant, St. Bonaventure, that Thou so lovest me that seemingly Thou dost hate Thyself for me: *Domine, in tantum dilexisti me, ut te pro me odisse videaris.* [5]

Let us come now to the love of the Holy Ghost, who is the Heart of the Father and the Son. When this divine Spirit formed the God-Man in the sacred womb of the Blessed Virgin Mary to give Him to us, did He know what we were to do? Did He know all the outrages and cruel deeds that men were to perpetrate against Him? Did He know that men would bend all their energies to destroy His wonderful masterpiece, the God-Man? Yes, He knew it well. Yet He did not hesitate to form Him in Mary's womb, to let Him be born for us, to appear in the form of a dove above His head during His Baptism in the waters of the Jordan, to make us recognize Him. He did not hesitate to lead His Son into the desert to do penance for our sins, to urge Him to preach the Holy Gospel and to proclaim to us the truths of heaven: *Spiritus Domini super me; propter quod unxit me, evangelizare pauperibus misit me.* [6] He did not hesitate to sacrifice Him on the Cross for our redemption: *Per Spiritum sanctum semetipsum obtulit.* [7] O love that hath no equal! O spirit of love and charity, bear with me when I say that seemingly Thou hast more love for man as sinner and culprit than for the God-Man who is the Holy of holies; for a slave of Satan than for the Only-begotten Son of God; for a firebrand of hell than for the King of heaven. O

[3] John 15, 9.
[4] Luke 22, 53.
[5] *In stimulo amoris,* part 1 [a] Cf. *Officium D. Cordis,* 7th day within the Octave, lesson 4.
[6] Luke 4, 18.
[7] Heb. 9, 14.

wonder without parallel! Who has thus bound Thee in a spell?
Pardon me, O adorable Spirit, if I speak thus, but is it not true
that the exceeding great love Thou hast for us seems to have cast
a spell over Thee as well as over the Divine Father and His Only
Son? How true is the saying, *Amare et sapere vix Deo conceditur!*

Even so do the Father, the Son and the Holy Ghost love us:
Sic Deus dilexit mundum; [8] even thus their divine Heart is a burning furnace of love for us.

What then shall we do to acknowledge such goodness? What
dost Thou ask of us, O God? Do we not hear His voice calling to us,
calling, calling, for so long? *Fili, praebe cor tuum mihi:* "My son,
give me thy heart." [9]

An eminent prelate, John Zumarraga, first Archbishop of Mexico,
in the Indies of America (New Spain), wrote to the Chapter of his
Order, assembled at Toulouse in 1532. According to the report of
Drexelius of the Society of Jesus, the Archbishop narrated that before the inhabitants of the city of Mexico were converted, they worshipped the devil through idols. He exercised such a cruel tyranny
that he obliged them to slaughter each year twenty thousand little
children, boys as well as girls, and to cut out the heart of each child
to be sacrificed to Satan on a fire of red-hot coals as incense. If in
Mexico City alone the hearts of more than twenty thousand young
children were immolated to Satan, you can imagine how many were
sacrificed to him every year throughout the whole kingdom of
Mexico.

We worship a God who does not ask of us things so strange.
True, He asks for our heart, but He has no desire that it be cut
from our body. He is satisfied if we give Him our affections, especially love and hate: our love to love Him above all things, with all
our strength; our hate to hate only sin. What is sweeter than to
love infinite goodness from which we have received every kind of
blessing? What is easier than to hate the most horrible thing in the
world and the sole cause of all our evils? Surely, if we refuse to
give our heart to the divine Saviour, who asks us constantly for

[8] John 3, 16.
[9] Prov. 23, 26.

it in a way so gentle and engaging, a heart moreover which belongs
to Him for countless reasons, all those pagans who sacrificed to the
devil the hearts of their dear children will rise up and condemn us
on the day of judgment. We shall be utterly cast into confusion when
the lawful King of our hearts points to the poor idol-worshippers
and says to us: "Behold these people who have torn out their children's hearts of living flesh to offer them to Satan, and you have
refused me the love of your hearts." We must not draw this reproach
upon ourselves. Let us give our hearts wholly and irrevocably to
Him who created them, who redeemed them, and has given to us
His own Sacred Heart so many times.

One of the fathers of the Society of Jesus, in his history of the
Crusades for the deliverance of the Holy Land, reports the following incident. In the year 1098, Geoffrey de la Tour, a nobleman from
Limoges and one of the most valiant of the Christian knights, one
day heard the roar of a lion, which sounded like a cry of pain.

Immediately he entered a near-by wood and ran to the spot from
which the roaring came. There he saw a horrible sight. A huge
serpent had wound its coils around the lion's body and legs, so that
it was powerless to defend itself. The serpent was darting its vene-
mous tongue, trying to strike the lion in a vital spot.

Geoffrey rushed forward with his sword and killed the snake without wounding the lion. The poor beast, finding itself freed and recog-
nizing his deliverer, came to thank the knight, by fawning and lick-
ing his feet. From then on, the lion attached itself to the man who
had saved its life. It followed him everywhere like a faithful dog,
never harming anyone, but ready to turn on a man who might
attack its master. But what is more wonderful is the sequel. When
Geoffrey sailed to return to France after the Crusade, the captain
of the ship would not allow the lion to come aboard, so the faithful
beast, plunging into the sea, kept on swimming in the wake of the
ship until its strength failed and it sank, thus showing that it preferred to drown rather than to be parted from its benefactor.

It should make us ashamed to have to learn the lesson of true
gratitude from a wild animal. Must we Christians be taught by
dumb beasts what we owe to God, our Sovereign Benefactor? O my

Saviour, Thou has freed me from the coils of the infernal serpent. Thou hast given Thy life to deliver me from the eternal death of hell, and enable me to enjoy everlasting happiness in heaven. Let me be all Thine; let me live only for Thee; let me follow Thee everywhere. May all the faculties of my soul be linked inviolably to Thy divine will. Let me have no thoughts but Thine; let me have no hate except for sin, no love but for Thee. Let me die many deaths rather than ever be separated from Thee.

CHAPTER 10

THE SACRED HEART OF JESUS IS OUR TREASURE HOUSE

THE ADORABLE HEART of our Saviour has been considered as a flaming furnace of love for us. We shall now see, first of all, that this heart is a vast treasure house containing infinite riches; secondly, that this wealth is ours; thirdly, the sacred use that we should make of it.

The Sacred Heart of Jesus is indeed an incalculable treasure, containing in itself all the marvelous riches of heaven and earth, in nature, grace and glory, in all the angels and saints, in the Blessed Virgin Mary, in the Godhead, in the Most Holy Trinity, and in all the divine perfections. St. Chrysostom says that the Blessed Virgin is an infathomable abyss of the boundless perfections of the Godhead: *Abyssus immensarum Dei perfectionum.*[1] How much more is this true of the adorable Heart of Jesus?

Moreover, His Heart is a most precious treasure house containing all the merits of His life, all the fruits of His divine mysteries, all the graces merited by His toils and sufferings, all His infinitely perfect virtues, all the gifts of the Holy Ghost wherewith He was endowed: *Requiescet super eum Spiritus Domini, Spiritus sapientiae et intellectus.*[2] In short, everything great, rich, precious and admirable in Creator and creatures, is stored in that incomparable treasure.

To whom does this marvelous treasure belong? It belongs to all of us and to each one in particular, since it depends only on us to take possession of it. By what titles and deeds does this treasure belong to us? By the title and deed of a gift. But who has given it to us? The Father of Jesus has given it to us in giving us His Son; and

[1] *In Hor. ani.*
[2] Isa. 11, 2.

He gives Him to us unceasingly, for His gifts are not transitory. *Sine poenitentia sunt dona Dei.*[3] The Son of God has also given it to us, time and time again, in giving Himself to us, and He gives it to us ceaselessly in the Blessed Eucharist. The Holy Ghost imparts this treasure to us incessantly. The Blessed Virgin also gives it to us continually, since she has but one heart and one will with her Son, her will is bound up in every gift of His.

It is, therefore, a clear fact that the loving Heart of Jesus is wholly ours, our very own Heart. Each of us can say with St. Bernard: "The Heart of Jesus is my Heart. I speak this fearlessly. For if Jesus is my Head, than what belongs to the Head belongs to me. Just as the eyes of my corporal head are truly my eyes, so the Heart of my spiritual Head is truly my Heart. What joy is mine! I am certain that my heart is one with Jesus." *Cor Jesu meum est, audacter dicam: si enim caput meum Christus est, quomodo quod capitis mei est non meum est? Sicut ergo oculi capitis mei corporalis mei oculi vere sunt, ita et spititualis Cor, Cor meum est. Bene ergo mihi, ego vere cum Jesu Cor habeo.*[4]

What would be the use of possessing an object of great value if the owner let himself die of hunger, thirst and cold? Or suppose he went into bankruptcy while still keeping the treasure? Similarly, what shall this greatest of treasures, the Heart of Our Lord, be worth to us if we do not draw upon its resources? God has given us His Heart to be our riches and our wealth, to draw upon to satisfy our obligations and to pay all our debts.

What are those debts? They are endless, for we are in debt to God and men, to the Creator and to all creatures. We owe the Creator five tremendous tributes: 1. adoration together with honor, glory and praise; 2. love; 3. thanksgiving for all the blessings that we continually receive; 4. reparation for our sins; 5. the gift of ourselves, seeing we belong to Him. Add to this, prayer, an obligation which is based on two principles: first, our infinite poverty and need, since we are nothing and have nothing of ourselves; secondly, the

---

[3] Rom. 11, 29.
[4] St. Bernard: *Tract on the Passion of our Lord*, Chap. 3. The treatise here mentioned by St. John Eudes is now attributed to St. Bonaventure.

fact that God is the supreme good ana the source of all good, and
that His infinite goodness inclines Him to pour out of His goodness
upon us to an infinite degree. He wills, and justly so, that we ask
Him for this in prayer.

Now, to pay all these debts, here is what must be done:

First, it is necessary to be in the state of grace. Secondly, when
you celebrate Holy Mass (if you are a Priest) or when you assist
at Mass (if a layman), but especially after Holy Communion, remember that you have the Sacred Heart there within your breast
and the Three Divine Persons, Father, Son and Holy Ghost. Addressing yourself first to the Father, speak to Him, with all possible respect
and humility:

"Holy Father, I owe Thee infinite honor, glory, love, adoration,
praise, thanksgiving and satisfaction; I also owe to Thee myself for
countless reasons. Of myself I have no means wherewith to pay all
these debts, being nothing and having nothing. But here is the divine Heart of Thy Well-beloved Son that Thou hast given me, which
I now offer to Thee to make satisfaction for my obligations to adore
Thee, to honor, praise and glorify Thee, to love Thee, to give Thee
thanks, to make amends for my sins, to give myself to Thee, and to
implore Thee by this same Heart, to grant me all graces of which I
stand in need. This is my treasure that Thou hast given me out of
the excess of Thy goodness; be pleased to receive it, O Father of
mercies, and graciously to reward Thyself by taking with Thine own
hands from this sacred treasure the wherewithal fully to satisfy and
pay all my debts."

After that make a similar offering to the Son of God, giving him
that selfsame treasure, His own Heart as well as that of His most
holy Mother, which is in a way but one with His, and which is more
pleasing to Him than all the hearts of paradise.

Perform the same act with respect to the Holy Ghost.

Next, remember the infinite obligations that you have to the
Mother of God, who gave you a Saviour with all the countless blessings that proceed from that marvelous gift and offer her the loving
Heart of her Beloved Son, in thanksgiving for all the favors that you
have received from that divine Mother. Offer her also that same

Heart in reparation, over and above, for all your negligences, infidelities, and failures in gratitude towards her. This is but a direction which she herself gave to St. Mechtilde, who, being anxious about her negligences in Our Lady's service, was counselled by the latter to offer her the most holy Heart of her Dearest Son. The Blessed Virgin assured the saint that this offering would be much more pleasing to her than any other pious devotions and practices.[5]

In addition, remember that you are still indebted to your Guardian Angel, to all the other angels, to your Patron Saint and to all the other saints, for their prayers and for the manifold helps they have given you. Consider, and offer to them all in general and to each one in particular your great treasure, as an act of thanksgiving, to satisfy for your shortcomings and to contribute to their accidental glory and joy.

Remember that you are also under obligations to your neighbor. You owe charity to all men, even your enemies; help to the poor, according to your ability; respect and obedience to your superiors, and the like. To satisfy all these obligations offer our Saviour His divine Heart to make up for the shortcomings of which you are guilty; ask Him to repay them for you and to give you all the graces necessary in the future to fulfil perfectly your obligations to your neighbor.

In the books of St. Mechtilde I find that when the saint was asked to implore Our Lord to grant a certain person a humble, pure and charitable heart, she acceded to his request and received this heavenly answer: "Let him seek in my Heart everything he desires and needs; and let him ask for them as a little child would confidently ask his father for anything he wants. When he desires purity of heart, let him have recourse to my innocence; when he desires humility, let him draw up from the deep well of my most humble Heart; there too let him drink in my love together with my holy converse, confidently taking to himself everything that is good and holy in that Heart, since I have given it wholly to my children."[6]

---

[5] Saint John Eudes does not mention where he obtained this fact. It was perhaps taken from a passage of the *Livre de la Grâce spéciale*, p. 1, chap. 46.

[6] *Livre de la Grâce spéciale*, p. 4, chap. 28.

This is the boundless and inexhaustible treasure that our Most Gracious Jesus has given us, in which we may confidently find everything that we need, so long as we possess that divine treasure in its richness. If we should lose it through sin, what a dreadful loss it would be! I am certain that if we fully understood it, we would realize that we would never sufficiently deplore such a great misfortune even though we were to live until the Day of Judgment and spend our time in weeping floods of tears and blood. If all the angels and saints were to descend from heaven to console us, they could never wipe away our tears. *Heu! quid perdidit, qui Deum amisit,* exclaims St. Augustine. "Alas! what hath he lost who hath lost God?" *Heu! quid perdidit, qui Cor Jesu amisit:* Alas! what hath he lost who hath lost the Heart of Christ, his Saviour? Who can understand the magnitude of that loss? Who can express it? Who can worthily deplore it?

Yet, after losing that infinite treasure, so many many times, you, O foolish man, are little affected by the deprivation. What sorrow should be yours! What tears of blood you should shed! How horrified you should be at your sins that have caused so dreadful a disaster! What fear of backsliding! How necessary to seek all the means possible to keep yourself from it! What would one not lose rather than to lose the loving Heart of our Redeemer! That gone, all is gone. Let us prefer to lose everything, our earthly goods, our friends, our health, even our life, rather than to lose the Heart of Jesus! O my Saviour, grant us that grace! Mother of Jesus, obtain it from thy Dear Son!

THE SACRED HEART OF JESUS LOVES US AS HIS FATHER LOVES HIM. WHAT WE SHOULD DO IN ORDER TO LOVE HIM

WE HAVE OUTLINED in the foregoing chapters numerous wonderful effects of the burning love of the Sacred Heart of our Saviour for mankind. But there is one effect of love that excels all the rest. It is expressed in the marvelous words rising from His divine Heart and spoken by His adorable lips: *Sicut dilexit me Pater, et ego dilexi vos:* "As the Father hath loved me, I also have loved you." [1]

Let us pause here a moment; let us weigh these words well: "I love you." How sweet are these words falling from the lips of the sovereign Lord of the universe! How encouraging, how helpful, how consoling! "I love you," our divine Saviour says to us. If an earthly ruler were to pay a visit to the house of the lowliest of his subjects and say to him: "I have come here expressly to assure you that I love you and that I shall let you feel the effects of love," what joy it would be for that poor man! Suppose an angel from heaven or a saint or the Queen of saints were to appear in a church thronged with Christians and were to proclaim in a voice that all could hear, to one member of the congregation "I love you; my Heart belongs to you." What transports of delight would thrill that privileged soul! Would he not die of joy? But here is much more than that. Here is the King of kings, the Holy of holies, the Only Son of God, the only Son of Mary, who has purposely come down here below from heaven to say to us: *Ego dilexi vos. Ego,* I who am the Creator of all things, I who rule the whole universe, I who possess all the treasures

[1] John 15, 9.

of heaven and earth, I who do whatsoever I will and I whose will none can resist, I love you. O my Saviour, what a rapturous word is this! Would it not be favor enough if Thou didst say to us: "I sometimes think of you; I look down upon you once a year; I have certain beneficial plans made for you?" But this is not sufficient for Thee. Thou dost wish to assure us of Thy love and affection for us, who are naught; for us, mere worms; for us, miserable sinners, who have so often offended Thee; for us who have so many times deserved hell: *Ego dilexi vos.*

But how does this adorable Saviour love us? Listen again to His sacred words: *Sicut dilexit me Pater.* I love you "as my Father hath loved me." I love you with the same Heart and the same love as that wherewith I am loved by my Father. Now what is that love wherewith the Divine Father loves His Son? It is a love possessing four great qualities, which are found in the love of the Heart of Jesus for us.

First of all, the love of the Father for His Son is infinite, that is, without bounds, limits, or measure; a love incomprehensible and inexplicable; a love as great as the very nature of the Eternal Father. Measure, if you can, the extent and the magnitude of that divine nature, and then you will measure the magnitude of that adorable Father's love for His Son; at the same time you will measure the greatness and the extent of the love of the Son of God for us, since He loves us with the same love as that wherewith His Father loves Him.

Secondly, the Father's love for His Son is an everlasting love filling all the spaces of eternity. The Eternal Father has never been without that love for His Son; He loves Him continuously, without intermission, and He will love Him eternally. O my Saviour, how it fills me with joy to see Thee loved as Thou dost deserve! The perfidious Jews, the devils and the damned hate Thee, but Thou art no less lovable, and the Adorable Father loves Thee more in a single moment than all those wretches could hate Thee in a thousand eternities, if that were possible.

Now, as the Father loves His Only-begotten Son with an everlasting love, the Son of God also loves us with an everlasting love. This means that all the spaces of eternity before and after are filled

with the love that He has for us. Hence, is it not true that if we had
existed from all eternity, we should have been bound to love that
gracious Saviour from all eternity? If we had a thousand years, ten
thousand, a hundred thousand, yes, even an eternity to live on earth,
should we not be bound to spend them in loving Him who loves
us with an everlasting love? Actually, we have at most a few decades
to exist on this earth, yet we waste them loving the world, the
degradation and the trifles of earth. Ah, how guilty we are to have
such ingratitude!

As our third reflection, we must remember that the love of the
Divine Father for His Son is a tremendous love filling heaven and
earth and even hell; in heaven, the Father loves this Son with the
hearts of all the angels and all the saints; on earth their mutual
love embraces all the hearts that belong to Him on earth; in hell,
the Eternal Father loves His Cherished Son who, with the other
Divine Persons, is present there, manifesting the same omnipotence
as in heaven.

Similarly, our Saviour loves us with an immense love filling
heaven, earth and hell; heaven, for He inspires all its citizens to
love us as themselves; He makes them sharers in the love He bears
us, and He loves us through them. He loves the earth in three ways:
1. He loves us wherever He has being on earth; 2. He creates, preserves and rules all things in the universe for love of us. This
thought prompted St. Augustine to utter these beautiful words:
*Coelum et terra, et omnia quae in eis sunt, non cessant mihi dicere
ut amem Deum meum:* "Heaven and earth and all things on earth
and in heaven cease not to bid me love my God." 3. He prohibits all
dwellers on earth, under pain of eternal damnation, to do harm,
either to our goods, our reputation, our person or anything belonging to us; and He commands them to love us as themselves.

The boundless love of our Redeemer fills heaven and earth, and
likewise hell; for He kindled the devouring fires of hell to inflame
our hearts with divine love. We are impelled to love Him, when we
consider that by our sins we deserved eternal torments if our Saviour
had not delivered us by His death on the Cross. O my God, Thou
dost love us everywhere, and we, ingrates, everywhere offend Thee.

Let it be so no more, but make us love and bless Thee everywhere: *In omni loco dominationis ejus benedic anima mea Domino.*[2]

In the fourth place, I could demonstrate to you further that, as the love of the Eternal Father for His Eternal Son is love in its essence, since He loves Him with His whole being, so also the love of the Son of God for us is love in its essence, since He is all heart and all love towards us and loves us with all His being. In other words, everything in Jesus, His divinity, His humanity, His soul, His body, His blood, all His thoughts, words, actions, privations, humiliations, sufferings, in short, everything that He is, has, and all His potentiality is bound up in loving us.

Here, I must mention one effect of His love that surpasses all the others. Louis Bail, a doctor of sacred theology, presents this fact in his learned and devotional work, *Affective Theology,*[3] and states that he found it in four passages of St. Bridget's writings approved by three Popes and two General Councils. Our divine Lord and His holy Mother revealed to St. Bridget that, while on the Cross, He suffered such keen, piercing, violent and terrible pains that His adorable Heart was rent, broken, and shattered: *Cor meum crepuit prae violentia passionis.* "My heart," says the adorable Saviour to the saint, "was utterly filled with pain, all the more because it was of a most fine and delicate nature; the pain went from my Heart into my nerves, from my nerves back to my Heart: it kept on increasing so that my death-agony was prolonged while I was thus immersed in suffering, I opened my eyes and saw my dearest Mother overcome by a sea of anguish and tears, which pained me more than my own sufferings; I also saw my friends overwhelmed with sorrow. With this torture my Heart was actually rent by the force and fury of the pain; and then it was that my soul went forth from my body." [4]

Those are the words of our Saviour to St. Bridget. In a later revelation He said: "There are few persons who can imagine with what pain I remained fastened to the wood of the Cross, my Heart being

[2] Ps. 102, 22.
[3] Part 3, Meditation 45.
[4] *Revel. extrav.* Chap. 51.

broken and shattered by its violence: *quando Cor meum crepuit.*" [5]

Let us now listen to the Blessed Virgin who revealed on two occasions to the same saint that, as the death of her Son drew near, His Sacred Heart was rent by the violence of the pain: *Cum Cor prae violentia dolorum rumperetur.*[6]

I also find a similar reference in the tenth exercise of the *Intimations of Divine Holiness* of St. Gertrude, where she thus addresses our Redeemer: *Deificatum Cor tuum in morte pro me rupit amor.* "Thy divine Heart was rent and broken in Thy dying, by the excess of Thy love for me. This made Thee suffer such violent tortures for love of me that Thy adorable Heart was broken by the force of the pain; so that I may say that Thou didst die of pain and love for me. This can be repeated by each one of us with equal truth." [7]

O Almighty God, who hath ever heard of such a death? O sinful man, wilt thou not open thy eyes to behold the love Thy Saviour has for thee? O heart of man, wilt thou not be touched by such burning love? Wilt thou not surrender? not be converted? Wilt thou not love one who hath such love for thee? *Filii hominum usquequo gravi corde?* [8]

How long will thy heart remain buried in the mud and slime of earth, in the mists and vanities of this world? Wouldst thou not love Him who is wholehearted in His love for thee and who, if thou wouldst but love Him, promises to give thee an eternal realm? That is all He demands of thee; for after saying, "I love you as my Father hath loved me," He adds: *Manete in dilectione mea:* "Abide in my love. If you keep my commandments, you shall abide in my love: as I also have kept my Father's commandments and do abide in his love." [9] Then He again says to us: *Haec locutus sum vobis, ut gaudium meum in vobis sit, et gaudium vestrum impleatur:* [10] "These things I have spoken to you that my joy may be in you, and your joy may be filled."

[5] *Ibid.* chap. 106.
[6] *Ibid.* book I, chap. 10; also chap. 26.
[7] *In Exercitio laudis et gratiarum actionis.*
[8] Ps. 4, 3.
[9] John 15, 9-10.
[10] *Ibid.* 11.

Wouldst thou, therefore, give great joy to thy Saviour and so act that thy heart may be always joyful and glad, thus beginning thy paradise on earth? Then love thy precious Saviour above all things, and thy neighbor as thyself. That is all that thou hast to do. O Jesus, I give Thee my whole heart. O Mother of Jesus, to thee also I give it entire, with all the hearts of my brothers and sisters in Christ; offer them, I beg, to thy Son, praying Him to take full, entire and eternal possession of them.

O Creator, I owe Thee my body and soul, because Thou hast given me Thy body and soul, Thy life and Thy very self. What do I owe Thee, and what shall I give Thee in return for all those priceless gifts? If I had millions of lives and gave them to Thee a million times over, each hour, that would be as nothing. Since I am so indebted to Thee that I cannot ever requite Thee, come Thyself as executor of my estate and take all that I have. I offer Thee all the faculties of my soul, all the feelings of my body, all my members, my whole heart, sacrificing myself entirely to Thy adorable will. I ask not for eyes except to contemplate what Thou dost will me to contemplate, nor for ears except to hear Thy divine words and to obey Thee. Let my tongue be torn from my mouth if I use it but to bless Thee; let my heart burst asunder rather than fail to love Thee. May I lose my memory, if it be not to remember Thee; and may my mind fail in all things, if it be not to know and to admire Thee. May my hands be cut off, if I use them not in Thy service. I ask not for feet except to seek and follow Thee. I will always exercise my will as Thou wouldst have me. Thy good pleasure is my sole desire. Do with me what Thou wilt, since for my sake Thou hast done with Thyself more than I would have dared to wish or to desire. I surrender myself entirely into the hands of God, my Eternal Father, who dost desire my welfare more than I do myself, who alone knows what is best for me and alone can obtain it for me.

CHAPTER 12

BEAUTIFUL WORDS ON THE LOVE OF THE SACRED HEART OF JESUS, TAKEN FROM THE THIRTY-SIXTH CHAPTER OF CHRISTIAN WELFARE [1]

"THOSE WHO HAVE WRITTEN on the devotion to Jesus Incarnate, living and dying for the salvation of all men, esteem it above all others, and assuredly with good reason. No matter what has already been said and might be said to demonstrate the excellence and the holiness of such devotion, it will never be praised according to its merits. Therefore, if you desire to be completely washed of your sins, delivered from all your vices and filled with virtue, cultivate a constant devotion to the person of your adorable Saviour. Lift up your heart and mind as often as possible, and plunge them into the loving Heart of Jesus, into that truly divine Heart, since, according to the Apostle, "in him dwelleth all the fulness of the Godhead corporeally," [2] and we are all able through this same Heart to have access to the Heavenly Father.

"Acquire the habit of recollecting your spirit within you, to draw it at the same time into the Heart of Him who has said: 'Come to me, all you that labor and are burdened, and I will refresh you.' [3]

"In fact, in the Heart of Jesus are to be found all virtues in their highest perfection. You will find there mercy, justice, peace, grace,

---

[1] St. John Eudes attributes the authorship of this work to Lanspergius, the saintly Carthusian of Cologne. The book was written by Dom Dominic, a Carthusian of Treves. The passages quoted by St. John Eudes were borrowed from a French translation of *Christian Warfare* published in 1671. Cf. Bainvel in *Etudes*, June 5, 1911, p. 606.

[2] Col. 2, 9.

[3] Matt. 11, 28.

eternal salvation, the source of life, perfect consolation, and that true light which lighteneth every man, particularly him who, in his needs and sorrows, comes there seeking help.

"Finally, you may draw from the Sacred Heart all that your soul desires and you will never win salvation or grace except from that source. It is a furnace of divine love, intensely burning with the fire of the Holy Ghost, which purifies, inflames and transforms into itself all those desiring to be united with this most loving Heart. It is in the adorable Heart that are hid all the treasures of wisdom and knowledge." [4] Therefore cling to it in such a manner that neither place nor company nor circumstance can prevent you from running to it as to a place of refuge where you will find only love and faithfulness, with the certainty that when all the hearts of men deceive and forsake you, and even though they fail in their response to you, the precious Heart of Jesus will never deceive nor abandon you. It is too faithful to commit an act of cowardice; it has too much love for you not to remember you; and the sufferings it endured for you will not permit it to overlook anything to achieve your salvation.

"If you wish to walk with safety in the heavenly way and enter by the true door, seek none other than this loving Saviour. Rest assured that you will never ascend to the knowledge of His divinity except by way of His sacred humanity, using His Cross as a prop to uphold your steps and sustain your weakness.

"If you wish to acquire even greater spiritual possessions, without much effort on your part, surrender yourself entirely to Him and He will surrender Himself to you. Offer Him all your good works in union with His excellence. Enter into partnership with Him in loving trust. He will be pleased with the exchange. In uniting your merits to His, you will have everything in common, and He will share with you His immense treasures. O profitable exchange! O unparalleled interchange! What man would not willingly give a small piece of copper for a large mass of gold? Who would not exchange a pebble for a precious stone? You will be able to effect this spiritual exchange if you join all your words, all your actions, all you thoughts

[4] Col. 2, 3.

and all your sufferings to those of Jesus. Thus, for instance, you will be able to say to Him: 'O my God and my Saviour, I offer Thee the slumber that I am about to take in union with that which Thou didst take while upon earth.' Or, when you receive some insult, say: 'O my adorable Saviour, I offer Thee this injury which I have just received, and I join it willingly to all the insults which Thou hast suffered on my behalf.'

"In this manner, your merits, although very small in themselves, joined to the infinite merits of your Redeemer, will be made more noble and will be absorbed in His, and, as it were, changed into them, as a drop of water is transformed when it falls into wine."

CHAPTER 13

THOUGHTS OF THE SERAPHIC SAINT BONAVENTURE ON THE LOVE OF THE SACRED HEART OF JESUS

THE SERAPHIC DOCTOR, St. Bonaventure, aflame with the love of Our Lord, says that the divine Heart is the gate of paradise, the joy of the elect, the beatitude of the angels, the treasure of divine knowledge and of eternal charity. The excessive love of that beloved Redeemer urged Him to open His divine side to give us His Heart and to make us dwell in its august sanctuary. Therefore the saint declares that he wishes to make his dwelling place in the Sacred Heart, to find there his repose and his delight. Whereupon he exclaims:[1] "Certainly, my Lord Jesus, even if Thou shouldst hate me, I should still have to love Thee, because Thou art my God. How much more must I do so, seeing that Thou dost love me so and dost pursue me to heap upon me Thy benefits? Thou hast such love for me that it would seem that Thou dost hate Thyself out of consideration for me.

"Didst Thou not consent, Thou Judge of the universe, to be judged and to suffer a most infamous and cruel death for love of me? O my God, what more couldst Thou have done for me? Certainly, Thou dost wish me to be surrendered unto Thee, since Thou hast given Thyself up to me. What constrained Thee to this sacrifice, O my God? Only Thy very great goodness and Thy immense charity, in order to enkindle us with Thy divine love. O sole desire of my heart! O sweetness and serenity of my mind! O flame in this brazier of my breast! O light and brightness of my eyes! O my soul! O my

---

[1] *Stimul. amor.*, Part I, chap. 1, and Part II, chap. 2.

life! O inmost recesses of my heart! O my joy and jubilation! Why am I not wholly transformed into love? Why is there anything in me but love? Thy love, O my Saviour, surrounds me on all sides, and yet I know not what love means.

"O Most Sweet Jesus, how wonderful is Thy love for men which will not suffer Thee to be separated from them! Is it not that love which, before Thou didst ascend into heaven, gave us the power to retain Thee, so long as we would, on our altars? Thou gavest us that power before going to meet death so that we might not fear losing Thee. Why didst Thou wish so to do, since Thou hadst the intent of sending us Thy Holy Spirit? Why didst Thou wish to abide always with man? Thou didst desire it to incorporate us in Thee, and to nourish us with Thy Precious Blood, so that being inebriated with Thy love we should have but one heart and one soul with Thee.

"O wondrous and inestimable power of love! It causes God to come down to earth and raises man to heaven. It unites God and man so closely that it makes God man and man God. The temporal becomes eternal, the immortal becomes mortal, and the mortal is made immortal. It causes the enemy of God to become His friend, and His slave to be adopted as His son.

"O love, what shall I render unto Thee who hast made me all divine? I live, yet not I, but Christ liveth in me. O love, Thy virtue is indescribable, Thou who transformest slime into God! What is more powerful than Thou? What is more gentle? what more pleasing? what more noble? O excellent love, that changest earth into heaven and makest me to form but one with my beloved! O desirable love, that dost intoxicate celestial lovers with sovereign delights! O my soul, if the voice of thy beloved makes thee melt into love for Him, why art thou not utterly inflamed and consumed when thou dost enter by the sacred wound of His side into the burning furnace of His loving Heart?"

CHAPTER 14

SEVERAL WONDERFUL THINGS ABOUT THE SACRED HEART OF JESUS, RELATED IN THE LIFE OF SISTER MARGARET OF THE BLESSED SACRAMENT, A CARMELITE NUN OF BEAUNE[1]

"THE SON OF GOD teaches that His members dwell in Him and He in them, that He is the true Aaron who bears the name of His people engraved in precious stones upon His breast, and carries them in the depths of His Heart out of His abundant love for them. We must not be surprised that He revealed to Sister Margaret of Beaune that He had placed her in the sanctuary where He universally receives all His chosen ones. When He chose to elevate her more and more in His grace, He drew her into His Sacred Heart where all those who love Him are to dwell everlastingly. He is a Father to whom all His children are dearer than the apple of His eye and He covers them under the shadow of His wings. His infinite charity for souls is pictured in countless ways, such as the beloved disciple resting against His Heart at the Last Supper, and the repose of the blessed in Abraham's bosom. He is a Shepherd, says the Prophet, who carries His lambs in His arms, holding them close to His breast. Hence the favor shown to Sister Margaret when, wishing to make her share in His heavenly delights, He lifted her into ecstasy and took her into His Heart.

"We have seen that God granted her holy conversation with the saints and angels and then raised her up to His throne in heaven.

[1] The author of the life, which appeared in 1655, is Father Amelotte, a priest of the Oratory.

Then He brought her still higher and, uniting her even more closely to Himself, He opened His own Heart and hid her in its Holy of holies.

"Thus He revealed His Heart as a vast and boundless furnace of love in which He enclosed her for days and nights. There were transfused so many graces at their source that her progress in perfection seemed greater in a single day than it had ever been for whole years at a stretch. That divine Heart, searing like a hot fire, consumed her imperfections. She was plunged into the abyss of charity so ardent that the heat issued forth and was felt outside of her body. The love of Jesus carried her away with such impetuosity that she was seen raised above the earth, fair and shining as a Seraph. At times she was bathed with love as in a fountain of sanctity. At other times she appeared to be tinged with innocence itself, and was fragrant with purity.

"She noted the twofold movement of dilation and compression of the Heart of Jesus, experienced by other Saints,[2] and understood that the Sacred Heart contracted as if to encompass the Holy Spirit, to love its Divine Father in His own name, to offer itself to Him as sacrifice, to humble itself before His majesty, to enter into His divine life, to unite itself to His adorable perfections, and to render Him all due homage. She understood that the Sacred Heart expanded to shed abroad its Spirit in all His members and to communicate to His Mystical Body, the Church, all the power of its vital warmth.

"She sensed in that loving Heart an endless, shoreless ocean of love for God His Father, a possession and an enjoyment of His divine goodness, a repose in His infinite bliss, a calm and peace passing all understanding, an incomprehensible treasure of all the virtues, which shone forth in a beauty, a nobleness, an expanse, and a splendor so great and inexplicable that there was enough to fill an infinite number of worlds thousands and thousands of times more vast than our planet.

[2] On the heart-beats of the Heart of Jesus, cf. St. Gertrude's *Herald of Divine Love*, Book III, chap. 51; Book IV, chaps. 4 and 24. Also St. Mechtilde's *Le Livre de la Grâce spéciale*, Part I, chaps. 5 and 20; Part V, chap. 32.

"Nevertheless, amid so much wealth and happiness, she saw that that divine Heart had been submerged, as it were, in the very deeps of pain and bitterness. It had been stricken down, heavy with sadness, on account of the sins of men whose gall and venom it had been obliged to taste. Unless it had been sustained by the Uncreated Word, it would have succumbed under the weight of our crimes.

"Despite the throbbings and the swoons occasioned by the constant horror of our sins, with all the struggles it had endured against the pains of death, she recognized in that most gracious Heart an unutterable transport of love for those who had caused it so many evils. As He fought against the apprehension of death, the strength and generosity of His love repulsed the spirits and the humors[3] which had drawn towards the center of His body, and caused it to break out in a sweat of blood.[4]

"She saw that wondrous Heart as a sacred palace where were born and nourished all the affèctions of the Saviour, His desires, His loyalties, His joys, and His sorrows. But among all those inexhaustible treasures of virtue and holiness, it was chiefly in the love, purity of heart, and innocence that she was allowed to share.

"Her lower faculties had been so consumed by the possession that God was assuming over her daily more and more, that she took little nourishment. She found in the Sacred Heart of Jesus a supernatural substitute which sustained her without eating and restored her strength more nobly than vital forces would have done. Sometimes it seemed to her that there flowed from that Heart through her

---

[3] The humors in old physiology are the four fluids: blood, phlegm, choler (yellow bile) and melancholy (black bile) conceived as entering into the constitution of the body and determining, by their relative proportion, a person's health and temperament. [Eng. Tr.]

[4] It is interesting to compare this passage on the sweat of blood with another taken from *Ancient Devotions to the Sacred Heart of Jesus by Carthusian Monks of the XIV-XVII Centuries,* Ref. London, 1926, p. 97: "In time of great suffering, the blood is concentrated in the heart in order to strengthen the principal member—hence the exterior parts of the body become pale—but in this exceptional case (Our Lord's), strength of mind so forcibly overcame natural weakness that it refused this aid, and sent back the blood to the outside as a sign of its readiness to be spilt without waiting for the hand of the executioner to shed it by force." [Eng. Tr.]

whole body a sacred liquid, now in the form of very sweet oil, now like purest milk, now like a balm filled with celestial fragrance, now like a pleasant manna fortifying not only body but producing marvelous effects in her soul as well.

"Worldly-minded people are far from understanding how a girl dwelling on earth could be hidden in the Heart of the Saviour. But the children of light, who feed on the life of the spirit, will readily conceive that it was not a transport of the body but only of the soul, and that her access to His Heart was a loving plan to associate her more closely with His innocence and His other virtues.

"Although the Son of God does not grant such special graces to every soul, it is conceivable nevertheless that there are many who, in the dark night of faith, enter as truly into His Heart and His affections as several saints who have been granted the luminous entrance perceptible to the intellect. Each of us has to raise himself humbly by the ordinary way of the Church, which is the way of faith. When we seek to love or adore God, to acquire a real sorrow for our sins, to sacrifice ourselves to the Eternal Father, we have no better way than to enter in spirit into the Heart of the Son of God. We must clothe ourselves with His holy dispositions, loving God in Him and with Him, detesting sin as He detests it, and uniting ourselves by faith with His perpetual sacrifice."

The author of the life of Sister Margaret of Beaune reports all the above details and enlarges on other points which I omit, because I wish to set forth only those that chiefly concern the adorable Heart of our Saviour. To Him be infinite honor, praise and glory, for all the graces, favors and blessings which His most benign and most generous Heart has dispensed and will dispense on earth and in heaven, in all hearts that love and shall love Him forever!

CHAPTER 15

A PIOUS AND LOVING EXERCISE ON THE SORROWS OF THE HEART OF JESUS AND OF THE HOLY HEART OF HIS BLESSED MOTHER

O GOOD JESUS, Lamb without spot, who didst suffer so many torments on Thy Cross, while beholding the virgin Heart of Thy dearest Mother plunged into an ocean of sorrows, teach me, I beg Thee, to accompany Thee in Thy sufferings and to feel Thy afflictions.

What a sorrowful sight to see those two Hearts of Jesus and Mary, two Hearts so holy, so innocent, so full of graces and perfections, so enkindled with divine love, so closely united to each other, and so compassionate towards each other! The holy Heart of the Mother of Jesus feels most keenly the terrible torments of her Son; the Only Son of Mary is wholly convulsed by the incomparable sufferings of His Mother. Jesus, the innocent Lamb, and Mary, His immaculate Mother, call to each other; the one weeps for the other, receiving no consolation; and the purer and more ardent their mutual love is, the more their sorrows penetrate and pierce.

O heart of stone! why dost thou not melt with sorrow and tears seeing that thou art the cause of the unutterable sorrows of that spotless Mother and that most gentle Lamb of God? What have they done to suffer so many afflictions? O wretched sinner, it is you and your abominable sins that are the executioners of those most holy and innocent Hearts. O Hearts most kind, pardon me and exercise upon me the vengeance which I deserve. Since creatures obey you, command them all to punish me as I deserve. Send me your sorrows and sufferings, so that, as I have been the cause of them, I may succor you in your weeping and pain. O Jesus, love of my heart, O

Mary, consolation of my soul, perfect image of Thy Son, stamp upon my heart a great aversion to the pleasures of this life, which thou hast spent in suffering. I am thine, belonging to thy house and thy service, although I am unworthy. Let me take no pleasure in this world except where thou dost find it. Grant that I may always bear thy sorrows in my soul, putting my glory and delight in being crucified with Jesus and Mary.

O most holy Virgin, how are all thy joys changed into sorrows? If they had been like those of the world, it would have been fitting that they should have suffered these changes. But, O Queen of angels, thou hast never taken pleasure except in divine things. God alone possessed thy Heart and nothing was able to satisfy thee but what proceeded from Him and led to Him. Thou hast had the joy of seeing thyself a Mother, the Mother of God; of bearing Him in thy sacred womb; of seeing Him resting on thy sacred bosom; of waiting on Him with thy most pure hands; of offering Him in the temple to His Eternal Father; and of seeing Him recognized and adored by Simeon the Just and holy Anna the Prophetess. All thy satisfactions, throughout the thirty years of thy life with Him, were divine, inward and spiritual. They were the jubilant, spiritual and interior delights with which thy most holy soul, enkindled with love for Jesus, thy Son and thy God, was raised and transported into His divine majesty. Thy holy heart, transformed and united to Him, received therefrom favors greater than all the ranks of heaven, since thy love exceeded that of all the Seraphim. O Lady and Queen of angels, what can one find in satisfactions so pure and holy, in joys so spiritual and heavenly, that could turn into sorrows? Can it be that the wretchedness and the servitude of the poor children of Eve exiled and banished from paradise, in whose sin thou hast never had part, have reached even to thee? Hath that exile, then, not yet ceased to be for thee a land of sorrows and a vale of tears?

O poor sinner, who would persuade yourself to find pleasure in this life which has only false and deceitful pleasures. Behold the sufferings of the King and Queen of heaven, and perish with confusion at the sight of your own disordered life and your aversion for crosses. The whole life of Jesus, who is innocence itself, is one continual suffering; the whole life of Mary, who is all holy and immaculate, is a perpetual Cross; and you, wretched sinner, deserving hell a thousand times over, you seek pleasure and comfort!

O Queen of angels, in all the years of the hidden life with thy Son Jesus, thou didst await the sorrows which were prophesied by holy Simeon, sorrows without parallel, since the magnitude of thy love was the measure of thy sorrow. When the time of the Passion of that loving Saviour had come, He took leave of thee to go forth to suffer, letting thee know that it was the will of His Father that thou shouldst accompany Him to the foot of the Cross and that thy Heart should be pierced with the sword of sorrow. St. John gave thee the warning, when he saw the time come for the divine Lamb to be sacrificed. Thou didst leave thy house to bathe Jerusalem's streets with thy tears. Thou didst find thy Son in the midst of an innumerable pack of human wolves and lions, howling and roaring at Him, shouting like madmen: *Tolle, tolle, crucifige, crucifige!* [1] Thou didst see Him, now no longer adored by kings, but held up to the people as a false king, blasphemed, dishonored, condemned to death, shouldering His Cross, led to Calvary, whither thou didst follow Him, bathed in thy tears and overwhelmed with sorrow.

Thou didst hear the blows of the hammer as He was being fastened to the Cross: they pierced thy Heart. Thou didst suffer unspeakable tortures, awaiting that dire hour of the Crucifixion. Thou didst see Him lifted up, while so many shouts and blasphemies were hurled at Him by the evil tongues of the Jews that thy blood congealed in thy veins. Thou didst spend these sad hours at the foot of the Cross, hearing the awful insults heaped by these wretches upon thy Lamb and seeing the frightful tortures which they made Him suffer, until at last thou didst see Him expire under such obloquy and suffering.

Whereupon they restored Him to thy loving arms, that thou mightest wrap His body in a shroud and bury Him and, just as thou hadst given Him at birth the first attentions, thou mightest now perform for Him the last rites; but with sorrows so heavy and anguish so sharp and desolation so penetrating to thy Mother's Heart that, if

[1] John 19, 15.

we are to comprehend anything of them, we should have first to comprehend the degree of thy well-nigh infinite love for thy Son. All things distressed thee. Wherever thou didst turn thou didst see only reasons for sorrow and tears. Thy Mother's Heart was rent the more with wounds bleeding and innumerable because thy Dear Jesus was also being wounded in Heart and body. It is true that thy faith was not diminished and that thy obedience kept thy Heart perfectly resigned to the divine will, but thou didst not cease to suffer inconceivable pain, even as thy beloved Son, in spite of His most perfect submission to all the commands of His Divine Father. Lastly, no heart with a lesser love than thine will ever be able to comprehend what thou didst suffer at that time.

When thy faithful servants and thy true friends consider these things, they give way to tears and are filled up with sorrow at seeing thy divine consolations changed into such cruel sufferings, thy most holy innocence falling prey to such inhuman sorrows. If they could only be torn asunder and consumed to console thee, most willingly would they suffer it. What a martyrdom of blood for the Heart of thy divine Lamb, the Only Son of God and thy Son, in seeing so clearly all the sorrows penetrating thy Heart, the desolation in which thou art, the anguish necessarily caused by Thy absence, and the fact that thou canst neither speak to Him nor He to thee, because no words can be found capable of appeasing such great sorrows!

O Father of mercies and God of all consolation what are those two Hearts that Thou art keeping thus crucified? Why dost Thou not succor Thy Only Son and Thy loving daughter? Why dost Thou not break the law that Thou hast made that one shall not sacrifice in the same day on Thy altar the Lamb and its Mother? And yet here, in one and the same day, at the selfsame hour, on the same Cross and with the same nails, Thou dost keep fastened the Only Son of sorrowing Mary and the virgin Heart of His most innocent Mother. Can it be that Thou dost care for the dumb animals, unwilling that the mothers should be sacrificed on the day they suffer the loss of their lambs, more than Thou dost for this most pure Virgin, grieving over the sorrows and the death of her divine Lamb? Thou dost will that she should have no other executioner of her martyrdom

than her tender love for her Only Son. Nevertheless, in the midst
of such cruel tortures, the sight of the sufferings of His most worthy
Mother were known to her Beloved Son even as He filled the cup
of her affliction and torture. Immortal praise and blessing, O my
God, for the incomprehensible love that Thou hast for sinners!
Thanksgiving, infinite and eternal, for all the works of that divine
love!

O Jesus, Only Son of God, Only Son of Mary, divine light of my
soul, I beseech Thee, for the infinite love Thou hast for me, to
enlighten my mind with Thy holy truths, to drive from my heart
the desire for the consolations of this life, and to instill into it the
desire to suffer for love of Thee. Thy love was the cause of Thy
torments. Thy love for Thy holy Mother and her love for Thee
were for her the source of a torrent of tribulations. How great my
blindness when I fancy I can please Thee by walking in any other
way! How long, O love, shall I be thus blinded and deceived? How
long shall this earthy man refuse to enter into Thy divine plans? Why
do I want life if not to employ it for Thee, as did Thy most holy
Mother, since Thou hast given Thy life for me on the Cross? What
more vivid enlightenment do I desire or need? O divine wisdom,
let Thy heavenly light everywhere be my guide; let the strength of
Thy love possess me utterly and work in my soul the transforma-
tion it operates in hearts obedient to it. I surrender myself, I offer
myself, I give myself all to Thee; may it be with a heart pure and
entire, O Lord. Take from me the pleasure I find in earthly things,
that I may find my pleasure only in loving Thee and suffering with
Thee.

O God of my heart, I adore Thee and render Thee infinite thanks
for turning to my advantage those sufferings which Thou endurest
in being confronted with those of Thy holy Mother, giving her to
me as Lady and Mother, and showing that Thou lovest me so much
that Thou desirest her to love me as her son in place of Thee. As
my heavenly Mother she will have compassion on me in my need
and will succor me, help me, protect, keep and govern me as her
child. Perhaps Thou hast not found, O my Redeemer, any greater
consolation for Thy most holy Mother than to give her evil and sinful

children to Thyself that she may use her power and charity to obtain their conversion and salvation. Blessed and praised be Thou forever that Thou hast willed that nothing should perish, but that all things should be used to cure my ills and to shower me with true blessings. Therefore, O good Physician, do not allow me, in the midst of such great remedies, to remain without relief. Receive me as Thine own and make me a worthy servant and a faithful child of this great Queen and kindly Mother.

O most holy Mother of God, remember that the pains which thou didst not suffer in the virgin birth of thy Only Son thou now dost suffer doubly at the foot of the Cross, in the spiritual birth whereby all sinners become thy children. I have cost thee so much, receive me as thy son. I am infinitely unworthy of it; perform for me, O most holy Virgin, the office of Mother, protecting me, succoring and guiding me in all things, and obtaining for me the grace of Thy Son, so that I, worthless and miserable child, may not be lost. O citizens of heaven, blessed and holy fruit of the spiritual maternity and the mother's Heart of this most pure Virgin, pray that she will always be a most kind Mother to me, and obtain for me from Jesus faithfully to serve and love the Son and the Mother in this world, and to be reckoned among those who shall bless and love them eternally in the other. Amen.

CHAPTER 16

EXERCISES OF LOVE AND DEVOTION TO THE SACRED HEART OF JESUS, FROM PHARETRA DIVINI AMORIS, "QUIVER OF DIVINE LOVE," BY LANSPERGIUS THE CARTHUSIAN

"Arouse and stimulate in your soul the devotion to the most gentle Heart of Jesus, that Heart entirely filled with love and mercy for you. Seek out the divine Heart frequently, with deep fervor and devotion, embracing it in spirit with the kiss of reverence and affection, and making it your dwelling-place.

"Ask God Almighty, through the Sacred Heart, everything you seek to ask. Offer to the Divine Majesty all your devotional exercises, through the Sacred Heart which encloses all the graces and gifts of heaven. It is the door through which you must go to God and God will come to you. To encourage yourself in this practice, and to benefit by it in stirring up true love for God, you should set up in a prominent place in your house a picture or statue of the Sacred Heart of Jesus.

"Whenever you look at it, remember your exile, your misery and your sins. Whenever you pass it, raise your heart to God. Even though you may speak no words, let your soul cry out. If you find that words are helpful, say a prayer that your heart be purified and your will perfectly united to the divine Heart and the will of God. If it helps your devotion, take the picture and kiss it reverently, directing your homage to the real Heart. Earnestly desire to imprint the real image of His Heart upon your own, surrendering your own mind and letting your heart draw into itself the spirit, grace and holiness of the vast abyss of virtue and sanctity abounding in the Sacred

Heart. It is very pleasing to God for you to give special honor to the adorable Heart.

"Have recourse to the most kind Heart of Jesus in all your necessities, and you shall receive all the consolation and help you need. Even if all men should deceive and forsake you, do not be discouraged. Abide in peace, for the Sacred Heart, so good, so faithful, so loving, can never deceive you and will never forsake you."[1]

PRAYER

"O most noble, most merciful, most gentle Heart of my faithful lover, of my God and Saviour, Jesus Christ, I beseech Thee to draw me to Thyself, and absorb my heart, all my powers, to Thy greater glory and for the accomplishment of Thy most holy will.

"O Jesus, most merciful Lord, I commend myself to Thy divine Heart, I resign myself and abandon myself entirely into Thy hands. I beg Thee also, O Most Gracious God, to take away this wicked heart, this impious and thankless heart, and to give me Thy Sacred Heart. Let my heart be according to Thy Heart and according to Thy holy will!

"O my Lord God, my Saviour and my Redeemer, take away all my sins and destroy in me everything displeasing to Thee; pour from Thy Heart into mine whatever will please Thee most. Wholly convert me and take full possession of everything within me, to use it according to Thy good pleasure and for Thine own sake. Unite my heart with Thine, my will with Thy will, so that I may never will and may never be able to will anything or in any other way than Thou willest and what Thou willest. O Sweet Jesus, O my God, let me love Thee with all my heart, in all things and above all things."[2]

ANOTHER PRAYER

"O my Most Loving Jesus, dearest spouse of my soul, I conjure Thee by the Sacred Heart pierced by a lance and rent by love, pierce, wound, break, enkindle and inflame my heart from that great brazier of love burning in Thy Heart, so that I may love Thee with all my

[1] *Pharetra divini amoris,* liber I, part 5.
[2] Lanspergius, *loc. cit.*

heart; that is, with the whole gamut of my desires and with a perfect will that shall consider only Thee, seek only Thee, and only aspire to Thee, loving Thee in all things and above all things." [3]

PRAYER TO THE SACRED WOUND IN THE SIDE OF JESUS, DRAWN FROM "THE ROSARY OF OUR LORD'S PASSION," BY LANSPERGIUS

"O my Most Loving and Gentle Jesus, I desire with all the affections of my heart, that all beings created and uncreated, should praise Thee, honor Thee and glorify Thee eternally for that sacred wound wherewith Thy divine side was rent. I deposit, enclose, conceal in that wound and in that opening to Thy Heart, my heart and all my feelings, thoughts, desires, intentions and all the faculties of my soul. I entreat Thee, by the precious blood and water that flowed from Thy most loving Heart, to take entire possession of me, that Thou mayest guide me in all things. Consume me in the burning fire of Thy holy love, so that I may be so absorbed and transformed into Thee that I may be no longer but one with Thee." [4]

ANOTHER PRAYER

"O Most Loving and Kind Father, in satisfaction for all my sins and for those of the whole world, and in reparation for my sloth, my tepidity, my neglect and my disordered love, I offer Thee that sacred wound in the Heart of Thy Son, the blood and the water which flowed therefrom, and the boundless love wherewith He didst love Thee. I beseech Thee that Thou wouldst pour from that sacred wound into my soul a love most pure, most intense, most perfect and eternal, wherewith I may love Thee with all my heart and bless Thee in all things and above all things. Grant that I may think of Thee only, that I may seek Thee only, that I be attached to Thee only, wish to please Thee only, and that I may wholly employ all the faculties of my body and soul to love Thee and glorify Thee." [5]

[3] *Ibid.*, liber II, part 5.
[4] *Loc. cit.*
[5] *Ibid.*, liber I, part 5.

CHAPTER 17

ANOTHER EXERCISE TO THE SACRED HEART OF JESUS, TAKEN FROM SAINT GERTRUDE'S EXERCISES ON PREPARING FOR DEATH

"O LOVE, thy flaming divine fire hath won me access to the beneficent Heart of my Jesus. O Heart overflowing with sweetness! O Heart filled with piety! O Heart surging with charity! O Heart distilling sweetness itself! O Heart full of mercy! Let me die of love in return for Thy love! O Heart of Jesus, my beloved, bury my poor heart in Thy treasure house! O costly pearl of my heart, summon me to Thy life-giving banquet, and although I am most unworthy, let me drink of the wine of Thy consolation, so that Thy divine charity may fill up my deficiency, and the abundance of Thy love may compensate for my lukewarmness and sloth!

"O precious love, how ardently I desire Thee now to offer up for me that divine Heart, that delightful fragrance, that incense of sweet savor, that august sacrifice, on the golden altar where the mystery of the reconciliation of the human race was accomplished, offering it in satisfaction for all the days of my life which I have let slip by without doing what I ought to have done for Thy love.

"O love, plunge my mind deep into that Sacred Heart as into a river, burying all my negligences and all my sins in the flood of Thy divine mercies. Let me find, in the Heart of Jesus, my understanding clarified, my affections purified, and let me have a heart free, detached and empty of all imperfections, so that, when love shall separate my soul and body at the hour of death, I may return my heart stainless to the hands of God. O all-loving Heart, whom I love above all things, Thou art the one whom my heart entreats with all its affections. Be mindful of me, I beg Thee, and may the sweetness of Thy charity restore and strengthen the weaknesses of my heart.

"O Thou eternal sweetness of my soul, O Thou beloved of my heart, whose holy face is full of charm and grace, whose Heart is so filled with sweetness as to make Thee infinitely lovable, must my thoughts wander from Thee? O God of my heart, gather up into Thyself all the disorders of my mind. O my beloved, wash Thou and wipe away, by the purity and the holiness of Thy divine affection and by the burning love of Thy pierced Heart, all the stains of my guilty heart and all the disorders of my imagination, so that Thy most bitter Passion may serve me as a sheltering defense at the hour of my death and that gentle Heart, broken for love of me, may be my eternal abode, since I love Thee alone more than all creatures in the world." [1]

[1] Exercit. VII, *Praepar. ad mortem.*

CHAPTER 18

COLLOQUY OF A HOLY SOUL, IN SOLITUDE, WITH THE SACRED HEART OF JESUS

O LORD, how delectable is the odor of Thy fragrance! It is my hope that henceforth its sweet delight will make me entirely forget the false pleasures and the vain delights of the world. May Thy sweetness draw me after Thee and in Thee so that, having abandoned all that binds me to earth, I shall follow Thee, run to Thee, flee to Thee and take up my abode in Thy loving Heart.

That divine Heart is a port of safety, where the soul is sheltered from the winds and storms of the sea of this world. In that adorable Heart there is a calm which fears neither thunder nor storm. Therein one tastes delight that knows no bitterness. One finds a peace that never brooks any trouble or discord. There one meets with a joy that knows no sadness. In that Heart one possesses perfect felicity, a gentle charm, an unclouded serenity and happiness unthinkable. That Heart is the first principle of all good, and the initial source of all the joys and delights of paradise.

Most Sweet Jesus, from Thy divine Heart, as from the inexhaustible source, all felicity, all sweetness, serenity, security, repose, peace, joy, contentment, charm and happiness flow into the hearts of the children of God. What good can there be, or how can there be any good thing, that does not proceed from Thee, my Jesus, who art essentially good, the real good, the sovereign good, the only good?

What a joy to drink from this divine spring! What happiness to be refreshed by the delicious waters of this fountain of holiness, which issues forth from itself like a torrent of delight and contentment! Ah, delightful a thousand times is the fragrant perfume of Thy heavenly virtues, whose fragrance is so delectable as to entice all men to Thy loving Heart! It invites them, it strongly attracts them and leads them into the sanctuary of that divine Heart. It never disappoints their hopes. On the contrary, it so fortifies and confirms them that they will never again depart, having found in that most kindly Heart, as on a bed of repose, the end of all their toils.

O Thou God of love, let the sweet fragrance of Thy divine perfumes, which are the wonderful virtues of Thy holy Heart, flow abundantly into the depths of my heart! Let that fragrance penetrate all the faculties of my soul, O one and only source of all happiness, so that being enticed by the sweetness emanating from Thee, it may become detached from self and perfectly united to Thee, that it may make its abode in Thy loving Heart, there to die to itself and no longer to live but in Thee and for Thee!

CHAPTER 19

FORTY FLAMES OR ASPIRATIONS OF LOVE OFFERED TO THE LOVING HEART OF JESUS

I. O wondrous Heart of my Jesus, what joy it gives me to behold in Thee all the grandeur, all the riches and wonders of all beings created and uncreated!

II. O divine Heart, first object of the Eternal Father's love, as well as of Thine own, I give myself to Thee to be plunged deep into the abyss of that love forever.

III. O adorable Heart of the Only Son of Mary, my heart is filled with joy to see that Thou hast more love for that Blessed Virgin than for all created things, and that her love for Thee is greater than for all created things together. I give my whole heart to that mutual love of Son and Mother.

IV. O most loving Heart of my Saviour, I offer Thee all that love which rises to Thee like a flame from the hearts of the divine beloved, begging them to kindle my heart with theirs.

V. O Jesus, lawful King and Lord of all hearts, be Thou the King of my heart, and let me be naught but heart and love towards Thee as Thou art to me naught but a Heart of love.

VI. O Jesus most good, whither shall I flee from Thy justice unless Thou hide me in Thy Heart?

VII. O wonderful Heart, Thou source of my life, let me live only in Thee and by Thee!

VIII. O most loving Heart, how dearly have I cost Thee, seeing Thou hast bought me with the last drop of Thy blood! How my heart would rejoice to give Thee its last drop!

IX. O Heart most good, Thou hast laden me with graces and favors. Let all my heart-beats be so many acts of love and praise of Thee!

X. O most gentle Heart, Thou hast always loved me. Let my heart not have a breath of life except to love Thee!

XI. O most charitable Heart, who hast died to give me life, let me live with Thy life and die by Thy death for love of Thee!

XII. O Jesus, Thy Heart is aflame with most pure love for me; let me also love Thee, not for any temporal or eternal interest, but purely and solely for love of Thee!

XIII. O my Jesus, Thy Divine Father hath put all things in Thy hands, and Thy love holds them ever open to give me all. May all that I have and all that I am be also entirely Thine forever!

XIV. O God of my heart, may the love which caused Thee to die for me make me also die for Thee!

XV. O Heart so great, what is there greater than Thou? Who shall tell me that there is aught, either on earth or in heaven, than that to which I have given my heart?

XVI. O Heart of Jesus, it is Thou who hast given me Jesus to be my treasure, my glory, my life, my all; let me also be all to Him!

XVII. O Only Son of God, how is it possible, being the Son of so good a Father, that Thou didst will to have so wicked a brother as I, who have so grievously offended Thy Most Loving Father?

XVIII. O Heart, full of wisdom and light, thinking of me and all the infinitesimal things that concern me, let my mind and my heart be also equally attached to Thee, and let me serve Thee faithfully in the smallest as well as in the greatest things!

XIX. O Heart most mighty, employ Thy divine power to destroy in my heart all that offends Thee!

XX. O Heart so great, loving me everywhere in Thy omnipresence, let me also love Thee everywhere and in all things!

XXI. O Heart most faithful in Thy love, who lovest Thy friends in adversity more than in prosperity, make me love Thee more in times of affliction than of consolation!

XXII. O Heart of the King of the lowly, veritable abyss of humility, crush in me everything that is contrary to that holy virtue, and make it rule absolutely in my heart!

XXIII. O Heart most obedient, who hast preferred to lose Thy life rather than disobey, make me love obedience, for without it I cannot please Almighty God!

XXIV. O Heart infinitely purer than the hearts of angels, the source of all purity, imprint on my heart a very special love of purity and a vivid horror of all that is contrary to it!

XXV. O Heart and furnace of flaming charity, destroy and consume in us all that is opposed to divine charity, and make it rule in all the children of God!

XXVI. O divine Heart, who could fathom the infinite hatred Thou hast for sin? Imprint it upon our hearts and make us hate nothing in the world but that infernal monster, which is the sole object of Thy hate.

XXVII. O Father of Jesus, love Thy Son Jesus for me. Make me share in that love Thou bearest Him!

XXVIII. O Jesus, love Thy Divine Father for me, and enkindle my heart with the love Thou hast for Him!

XXIX. O adorable Spirit, who art all love and charity, do Thou love my Most Gracious Father and my Most Loving Jesus for me, and transform my whole heart into love for Them!

XXX. O Jesus, Only Son of God and Only Son of Mary, love Thy divine Mother for me, and enkindle my heart with Thy wondrous love for her.

XXXI. O Mother of love, do thou love Thy Jesus and my Jesus for me, and make me share in the love Thou hast for Him.

XXXII. O blessed St. Joseph, St. Gabriel, St. Joachim, St. Anne, St. John the Baptist, St. John the Evangelist, St. Lazarus, St. Mary Magdalene, St. Martha, all ye holy apostles and disciples of Jesus, all ye holy martyrs, all ye holy priests and levites, all ye holy virgins and all ye other saints, especially ye beloved of the Hearts of Jesus and Mary, do ye love Jesus and Mary for me, and pray them to model me after their example and to number me among the children of their Heart, and to associate me in your love for them forever and ever.

XXXIII. O my Jesus, since Thy Father hath given me all in giving me Thee, all the hearts of the universe belong to me; therefore I include them all in the desire to love Thee with all the love of which they were capable when Thou didst create them to love Thee.

XXXIV. O my Jesus, hast Thou not said that Thou didst come to cast fire upon the earth, and that Thou hast no greater desire than to kindle all hearts? How is it then that the whole earth is full of hearts like ice? Sin is the sole cause of man's frigid soul. O cursed sin, how gladly would I be reduced to nothingness that you might be annihilated in every soul!

XXXV. O Heart of my Jesus, great furnace of love, send Thy sacred flames into all hearts of the universe, to enlighten them with heavenly fire and enkindle them with Thy divine sparks!

XXXVI. O Good Jesus, who hast so loved the Cross for love of me, that Thy Holy Spirit calls the day of Thy great sufferings the day of Thy Heart's joy, make me love and embrace with my whole heart all the crosses that are in store for me out of love for my most precious Crucified!

XXXVII. O most loving Hearts of Jesus and Mary, who are but one Heart in the unity of mind, will and affection, make your most unworthy child have but one heart with you and with all hearts that are yours!

XXXVIII. O Heart of Jesus, the Father of mercies and the God of all comfort hath given Thee to me and Thou art really my heart. Do Thou love for me everything that I should love and in the way that my God wills that I should love it.

XXXIX. O Heart of Jesus and Mary, inestimable treasure of manifold good, be my one treasure, my refuge and my protection! To you I have recourse in all my needs and necessities. When the hearts of all men deceive and abandon me, I have full confidence that the most precious and faithful Heart of my Loving Jesus and of His most sweet Mother will not deceive me and never will abandon me.

XL. Attend and hear, O vast furnace of love! It is but a tiny straw asking most humbly and earnestly to be immersed, absorbed, lost, swallowed up and consumed in Thy sacred flames for ever and ever!

LIVE JESUS AND MARY

MEDITATIONS

Meditations

FOR THE FEAST OF THE SACRED HEART OF JESUS

FIRST MEDITATION
The Vigil of the Feast
*Dispositions Required for the Worthy
Celebration of This Feast*

FIRST POINT

THE FIRST DISPOSITION FOR THE FEAST OF THE SACRED HEART
OF JESUS IS A BURNING DESIRE TO CELEBRATE IT DEVOUTLY

CONSIDER that the adorable Heart of Jesus is the principle and source
of His Incarnation, Birth, Circumcision, Presentation in the Temple,
and of all the other mysteries and states of His life as well as of all
His thoughts, words, deeds and sufferings for our salvation. His heart
burning with love prompted Him to perform all these things for us.
Thus it is that we owe honor and love to this most amiable Heart for
countless reasons, and to show our affection we must celebrate this
Feast with all possible devotion.

Let us offer our hearts to the Holy Ghost, and earnestly beg Him
to enkindle us with a burning desire to celebrate the Feast of the
Sacred Heart with as much devotion as though we were to celebrate
it only once on earth. This great desire constitutes the first requisite in
preparation for this solemn Feast.

The Second Disposition is Humility

The second disposition is one of deep humility. We must acknowledge our infinite unworthiness to take any part in the celebration of such a holy solemnity:

1. Because it belongs to heaven rather than to earth; and because the Feast of the Sacred Heart of Jesus is a feast of the Seraphim rather than of sinful men.

2. Because, through our negligence, God's blessings have not borne the fruit they should have in our souls, although we have celebrated this Feast many times.

The divine Heart is the source of every grace that we have received from heaven throughout our lives; yet our ingratitude and faithlessness have rendered these precious gifts fruitless and ineffectual.

May these thoughts inspire us to profound humility. Let us enter again and again into a true spirit of penance, which will prompt us to detest our sins, to excite genuine contrition in our souls, and to make a good confession to purify our hearts so that we may become worthy recipients of the light and grace necessary for a holy celebration of this Feast.

The Third Disposition is Union With the Three Divine Persons of the Blessed Trinity, the Blessed Virgin Mary, and the Angels and Saints

As the third disposition we must offer ourselves to the Father, the Son and the Holy Ghost, to the Blessed Virgin Mary, to all the angels and saints, especially to our guardian angels and our patron saints. We must implore them to prepare our hearts and to invite the heavenly Court to celebrate this Feast with us. Let us ask them to make us their associates and sharers in their ardent love for the most adorable Heart of Jesus.

Ejaculatory prayer: Thanks be to Thee, Lord Jesus, for the ineffable gift of Thy Sacred Heart.

Gratias tibi, Domine Jesu, super inenarrabili dono Cordis tui.

SECOND MEDITATION
The Day of the Feast
The Gift of the Sacred Heart of Jesus to Us

FIRST POINT

JESUS HAS GIVEN US HIS SACRED HEART

ADORE and consider our most lovable Saviour in the excess of His goodness and in the generosity of His love towards us. Consider attentively His boundless beneficence. He has given us life and all the benefits that spring from the gift of life. He has given us His Eternal Father to be our True Father, His most holy Mother to be our dear Mother, His angels to be our protectors, and His saints to be our advocates and intercessors. He has given us His Church, our second Mother, together with all the sacraments of His Church for our salvation and sanctification. He has given us all His thoughts, words, actions and mysteries, all His sufferings, and His very life which He spent and sacrificed for us, even to the last drop of His Precious Blood.

Moreover, He has given us His most lovable Heart, the principle and source of all other gifts. The charity of His divine Heart impelled Him to emanate from the adorable bosom of His Father, and come upon earth so that He might give us all these priceless favors. This Heart, humanly divine and divinely human, merited these graces by His sufferings, endured for us on earth.

SECOND POINT

WE SHOULD GIVE OUR HEARTS TO JESUS

How shall we repay our loving Redeemer for so much love? We must render love for love. In return for the gift of His Sacred Heart we must give Him our hearts without reserve. To return Our Lord love for love, we must offer our love wholly and completely to Him. He has given us His Heart for all eternity; we must give Him ours forever. He has given us His Heart with infinite love; let us give Him ours in union with His infinite love. He is not satisfied with giving us His own Heart, He has also given us the Heart of His Eternal Father, the heart of His most holy Mother and the hearts of all His angels and saints. He even gives the hearts of all mankind who are commanded under pain of eternal damnation to love us as He has loved us: *Hoc est praeceptum meum ut diligatis invicem sicut dilexi vos.*[1]

Let us also offer Him in thanksgiving the Heart of His Eternal Father, the Heart of His holy Mother, the hearts of all the angels and saints and of all men; these are ours to give as though they belonged to us. St. Paul assures us that with the gift of His Son the Eternal Father has given us all things: *Omnis cum ipso nobis donavit,*[2] and that all things are ours: *Omnia vestra sunt.*[3] But above all let us offer Him His own Heart; He has given it to us; therefore it is ours and is the most acceptable offering we could make to Him. It is His own Heart and at the same time the Heart of His Eternal Father, one by unity of essence. It is also the heart of His most holy Mother, whose Heart is one with His by unity of will and affection.

Ejaculatory prayer: Let us give thanks to the Sacred Heart of Jesus for his ineffable gifts.

Gratias infinitas super inenarrabilibus donis ejus.

[1] John 15, 12.
[2] Rom. 8, 32.
[3] I Cor. 3, 22.

THIRD MEDITATION

The Gift of This Feast Is a Great Favor from Our Lord

EXCELLENCE OF THE FEAST OF THE SACRED HEART

LET US ADORE the incomprehensible goodness of our most loving Redeemer in giving us this holy Feast. It is, indeed, an extraordinary grace.

To understand it at all adequately, we must remember that the feasts celebrated by Holy Church during the course of the year are fountains of sanctification and blessings, but this Feast is a veritable sea of grace and holiness. The Feast of the Most Sacred Heart of Jesus constitutes an immense ocean of feasts, because it commemorates the principle of all the other feasts celebrated by Holy Church. It also is the festival of the prime source of everything that is great, holy and venerable in each of the other feasts.

It is our duty, then, to render infinite thanks to our Saviour for His goodness, and to invite the Blessed Virgin, all the angels and saints and all creatures to unite with us to praise, bless and glorify Him for this ineffable favor.

We should also dispose our souls to receive the graces He wills to communicate to us during the solemnity of this wonderful Feast. We must make a strong resolution to do everything in our power and to employ all our affections and every means possible to continue to celebrate it appropriately and devoutly during the Octave.

OUR DUTIES TO THE SACRED HEART OF JESUS

Why has the King of all hearts given us this Feast of His most lovable Heart? Solely that we may perform our duties to Him. We have four principal duties to fulfil.

The first duty is adoration. Let us adore the Heart of Jesus with all our heart and all our strength. It is infinitely worthy of adoration because it is the Heart of God, the Heart of the Only-begotten Son of the Eternal Father and of God made man. Let us adore this precious Heart, offering It all the adoration ever accorded to It in heaven and on earth. O my Saviour, may the whole universe unite in adoration of Thy divine Heart! I willingly consent to be reduced to nothingness now and forever, by means of Thy grace, so that the Sacred Heart of Jesus may be incessantly adored by the whole universe.

Our second duty is to praise, bless, glorify and thank His infinitely generous Heart for Its tremendous love for the Eternal Father, His most holy Mother, all the angels, all the saints, and all creatures, especially ourselves. Let us also thank Him for all the gifts, favors and blessings poured out from this immense sea of graces upon all things created, particularly upon us. O most sublime Heart, I offer Thee all the praise, glory and thanksgiving rendered Thee in heaven and on earth, in time and eternity. May all hearts praise and bless Thee forever!

The third duty is to ask pardon of His kind Heart for all the sorrow and suffering endured for our sins, and to offer in reparation all the satisfaction and joys given to Our Lord by His Eternal Father, by His Blessed Mother and by all ardent and faithful hearts. Let us accept out of love for the Sacred Heart all the trials, sorrow and affliction which may come upon us.

The fourth duty is to love this divine Heart with all possible affection and fervor in the name of those who do not love It and to offer It the entire love of all hearts that belong to It. O Heart all-lovable and all-loving, when shall I begin to love Thee as I should?

I am under countless obligations to love Thee; yet, alas, I realize that I have not even commenced. Grant me the grace to begin straightway to love Thee. Destroy in my heart whatever is displeasing to Thee and establish instead the reign of Thy holy love.

Ejaculatory prayer: God of my heart, my portion, Jesus forever.
   Deus cordis mei, pars mea, Jesus in aeternum.

FOURTH MEDITATION

The Sacred Heart of Jesus Is Our Refuge, Our Oracle, and Our Treasure

THE SACRED HEART OF JESUS IS OUR REFUGE

IN THE FEAST we are celebrating our most loving Saviour has given us His Heart, not only as the object of our homage and adoration, but also as our refuge and our shelter. Let us resort to this haven in all our undertakings and seek therein our consolation in our sorrows and afflictions. Let us place ourselves in the shadow of its protection against the malice of the world, against our own passions, and the snares of the devil; let us retire to this shelter of goodness and mercy to shield ourselves from all the perils and miseries of life. Let us seek refuge in the Sacred Heart, in the tower of strength, where we may escape the vengeance of divine justice for our sins which caused the death of the very Author of life. May this most benign and generous Heart be our shelter and our refuge in all our necessities!

SECOND POINT

THE SACRED HEART OF JESUS IS OUR ORACLE

Our divine Lord has given us His Heart also to be our oracle. How much more valuable is this gift than the first oracle which was placed in the tabernacle of Moses and afterwards in the temple of

93

Solomon! The first oracle was confined to one place, but ours is to be found wherever our Saviour is present. The former was in existence but a few centuries; ours will last until the end of time. The oracle of Old Law spoke by the voice of an angel, but the oracle of the New Law is the very voice of Christ Himself. O Jesus, Thou dost speak heart to heart, teaching us Thy will, resolving our doubts, smoothing our difficulties when we have recourse to Thy Sacred Heart with faith, humility and confidence.

If we wish to know what God asks of us upon different occasions, if we have a difficult task to undertake, if we are in doubt or perplexity, let us have recourse to the Heart of Our Lord, celebrating Holy Mass in His honor or else receiving Holy Communion. Thus we shall experience the consoling effects of His goodness.

THIRD POINT

The Sacred Heart of Jesus is Our Treasure

Our most lovable Redeemer has also given us His most loving Heart to be our treasure. It is an immense and inexhaustible treasure which enriches heaven and earth with infinite blessings. Let us draw from this treasure whatever we need to pay our infinite debts to divine justice for our failings. Let us offer the most Sacred Heart in satisfaction for our numberless sins, offenses and negligences.

If we lack some virtue, we must draw upon the treasure house of all virtues, the Sacred Heart of Jesus. If we need humility, let us beg Him to impart to us a share in His profound humility. If we need charity, let us implore Him by His most ardent charity to give us perfect charity. Likewise we may take each virtue in turn.

When we need a special grace to meet certain circumstances, let us ask Our Lord through His most benign Heart to grant it to us from our treasure house.

If we desire to help the souls in purgatory, let us offer God our precious treasure that He Himself may take from it the price due His justice.

When the poor beg for alms, we should ask the Sacred Heart the grace to respond to their appeal and give them a share in our heavenly treasure by saying this prayer: "O most benign and generous Heart of Jesus, have mercy upon all those who suffer."

When people ask to be remembered in our prayers, or make any request of us, we should lift up our hearts to Christ, our treasure, saying with true confidence and with deep humility: "O loving Saviour, arouse in me the feelings of Thy charitable Heart toward all who come to me for help."

The heart of every man is attached to whatever is his treasure. Let us so direct our life that all the affections of our heart may be concentrated on the greatest of all treasures, the most amiable Heart of Jesus.

Ejaculatory prayer: O God of my heart, my love, Jesus forever.
   Deus cordis mei, amor meus, Jesus in aeternum.

FIFTH MEDITATION

The Sacred Heart of Jesus Is the Perfect Model and Rule of Our Lives

THE SACRED HEART OF JESUS IS OUR PERFECT MODEL

WE SHALL never be able to understand adequately and esteem at its full value the inconceivable grace Our Lord has granted us in giving us His divine Heart. Let us picture a man who was such a favorite of the king that he could truthfully say: "The king's heart belongs to me." What happiness and joy to be so favored! But we have infinitely more than the heart of an earthly king. We have the Heart of the King of kings, who loves us so ardently that each one of us can truly say: "The Heart of Jesus belongs to me."

Yes, this admirable Heart is mine. It is mine because the Eternal Father has given it to me; it is mine because the Blessed Virgin has given it to me; it is mine because He Himself has given it to me, not only to be my refuge and shelter in my needs, to be my oracle and my treasure, but also to be the model and rule of my life and of my actions. I wish to study this rule constantly so as to follow it faithfully.

I must consider what the Heart of Jesus hates and what it loves, in order to hate only what it hates and love only what it loves. The only thing it hates or ever shall hate is sin. Did His gentle Heart feel any hatred for the miserable Jews who persecuted Him so unjustly or for the executioners who treated Him so cruelly? No, He never experienced the emotion of hatred. On the contrary, He besought His

Eternal Father to pardon His executioners and even excused the most outrageous of all crimes.

I wish to follow the Divine Rule for love of Thee, my Saviour. I will hate nothing but sin; I will love all that Thou lovest, even my enemies. With the help of Thy grace I will do all the good I can to those who seek to harm me.

SENTIMENTS THAT SHOULD FILL OUR HEARTS IN IMITATION OF THE HEART OF JESUS

My rule tells me that I must have in my heart what is in the Heart of Our Lord: *Hoc sentite in cordibus vestris quod et in Christo Jesu.* [1] These sentiments are:

1. His affection for the person and will of His Eternal Father. He so loves His Father that He has sacrificed Himself and is still prepared to sacrifice Himself a hundred thousand times for His glory. His love for the divine will is so great that never once in the course of His life did He prefer His own will but found His entire satisfaction in doing His Father's will: *Meus cibus est ut faciam voluntatem ejus qui misit me.* [2]

2. Another sentiment of His Heart is horror of sin. He hates evil to such a degree that He delivered Himself to the wrath of His enemies and to the torments of the Cross to crush the infernal monster.

3. A third sentiment is His esteem for the Cross and for suffering which He loves so tenderly that the Holy Ghost speaking of His Passion called it the day of His Heart's joy: *In die laetitiae cordis ejus.* [3]

4. His love for His Mother is the fourth sentiment of His divine Heart. He loves her alone more than all His angels and saints together.

[1] Phil. 2, 5.
[2] John 4, 34.
[3] Cant. 3, 11.

5. There is also a sentiment of charity for us. He so devotedly loves us that "it seems," says St. Bonaventure, "that He hates Himself for us." *In tantum me diligis, ut te pro me odisse videaris.*

6. Lastly there is the sentiment of His Heart towards the world. He hates it as something accursed and outcast, openly declaring that it has no part in His prayers: *Non pro mundo rogo,*[4] and that His children are not of the world: *De mundo non sunt sicut et ego non sum de mundo.*[5]

Such are the Divine Rules I wish to observe for love of Thee, my Saviour. I long to love God with all my heart, with all my soul and with all my strength. I long also to find my satisfaction in following in all things and everywhere His most adorable will. I long so to abominate all kinds of sin, that by means of Thy holy grace I may rather die than ever consent to it. O my Jesus, make me love crosses and afflictions that I may seek all my joy in them for the love of Thee and that I may say with St. Paul: *Repletus sum consolatione; superabundo gaudio in omni tribulatione nostra.*[6] Make me a sharer in Thy very great love for Thy holy Mother that she after Thyself may be the center of my veneration and fervent devotion. Impress upon my heart the hatred Thou hast for the world. Make me detest it as a veritable antichrist which is always opposed to Thee and has crucified Thee so relentlessly. Grant, I beseech Thee, O God of my heart, the grace, that for the love of Thee I may always preserve in my soul an entire and perfect charity for my neighbor. This is the rule of rules: *Quicumque hanc regulam secuti fuerint, pax super illos.*[7]

Ejaculatory prayer: O Sacred Heart of Jesus, law and rule of our heart.

   O Cor Jesu, lex et regula cordis nostri.

[4] John 17, 9.
[5] John 17, 16.
[6] 2 Cor. 7, 4.
[7] Gal. 6, 16.

SIXTH MEDITATION

Jesus Has Given Us His Sacred Heart to Be Our Heart

THE SACRED HEART OF JESUS IS GIVEN TO US TO BE OUR HEART

THE SON OF GOD gives us His Heart not only to be the model and rule of our life, but also to be our heart, so that by the gift of this Heart, immense, infinite and eternal, we may fulfil all our duties to God in a manner worthy of His infinite perfections. We have three obligations in regard to God: 1. To adore His divine grandeur; 2. To render Him thanks for His unspeakable gifts; 3. To implore Him to grant through His divine generosity all the necessities of soul and body.

How are we able to discharge these duties in a manner worthy of God? We are utterly unable to do so. Even if we had the minds, the hearts and the strength of all angels and men, and if we were to use them to adore, thank, and love God and to satisfy His divine justice, we could accomplish absolutely nothing to discharge our obligations as creatures of God. We have, however, received from our Divine Saviour the gift of His adorable Heart which is the perfect means of fulfilling all these duties. We should employ the Sacred Heart as if it were our own heart, to adore God fittingly, to love Him perfectly, and to satisfy all our obligations adequately so that our homage and love may be worthy of His supreme majesty. Eternal and infinite thanks be rendered Thee, O Good Jesus, for the infinitely precious gift of Thy divine Heart. May all the angels, saints, and all creatures bless Thee forever!

SECOND POINT

How We Should Make Use of the Sacred Heart of Jesus

What happiness and what wealth to possess the divine Heart of Jesus! What a treasure to have at our disposal! How great is our obligation, O my Saviour, because of Thy incomprehensible goodness! Thou dost ask the Eternal Father to make us one with Him and with Thee, as Thou and He are but one. Consequently Thou dost wish to be one in heart with Thee and with Thy Adorable Father. Thou hast willed to be our Head, and hast willed us to be Thy members and to have but one heart and one spirit with Thee. Thou hast made us children of Thy Heavenly Father; Thou hast given us Thy divine Heart, so that we may love the Father with Thy very own Heart. Thou hast assured us that the Adorable Father loves us even as He loves Thee. *Dilexisti eos sicut et me dilexisti.*[1] Thou dost love us with the same Heart with which the Father loves Thee: *Sicut dilexit me Pater et ego dilexi vos.*[2] Thus Thou dost give us Thy Heart that we may love the Father and Thyself with the same heart and with the same love with which Thou lovest us. We should, therefore, employ Thy Sacred Heart to offer Thee our adoration, praise, thanksgiving, and all our other duties with a reverence and love worthy of Thy infinite greatness.

What must we do to employ the great Heart that God has given us? We must do two things. First, whenever we adore, praise, thank and love God, or practise some virtue, or accomplish some action for His service, we must renounce our own heart which is poisoned with the venom of sin and of self-love. Secondly, we must unite ourselves to the love, charity, humility and all the holy dispositions of His Sacred Heart, so that we may be worthy to adore, love, praise, serve and glorify God with the Heart of God.

O my Saviour, extend the power of Thy eternal arm to separate me from myself and unite me to Thee. Pluck out my miserable heart and

[1] John 17, 23.
[2] John 15, 9.

replace it with Thine own, enabling me to say: *Confitebor tibi, Domine, in toto corde meo.*[3] I will praise Thee and love Thee, my Lord, with my whole heart—with the great Heart of Jesus, which is my own heart.

O Heart all lovable and all loving of my Saviour, be Thou the Heart of my heart, the soul of my soul, the spirit of my spirit, the life of my life and the sole principle of all my thoughts, words and actions, of all the faculties of my soul, and of all my senses, both interior and exterior.

Ejaculatory prayer: O Heart all mine, I possess all things in possessing Thee!

O *Cor meum, Cor unicum, in te mihi sunt omnia!*

[3] Ps. 9, 2.

SEVENTH MEDITATION
The Most Profound Humility of the Sacred Heart of Jesus

SELF-ABASEMENT OF THE SACRED HEART OF JESUS

HUMILITY IS a virtue including an infinity of degrees because there are innumerable sources of humiliation. There are, however, three principal ones. The first is our nothingness which is a bottomless abyss of abjection and humiliation. The second is the infinite grandeur of God, for all greatness carries with it lowliness in those who are inferior to it, and the greater the elevation, the greater is the demand of humiliation on the part of the inferior. That is why the supreme greatness of the majesty of God should impress on created beings an abasement infinite in itself. The third principal humiliation is sin. The least of our sins is an infinite abyss of abasement, and God could justly annihilate us for our smaller faults.

Self-abasement is the first effect that humility should produce in our heart. It operated prodigiously in the Heart of our divine Saviour because Jesus, as man, understood very clearly that He Himself was nothing and of Himself had only nothingness.

Secondly, His very clear perception of the immense grandeur of God held Him continually in a state of incomprehensible lowliness.

Thirdly, He realized that He was a Son of Adam, and that original sin is an immense ocean of sin. It is the very fountainhead of all the sins past, present and future in the whole world, even if it should last for thousands of years more. Jesus understood that if He had been merely man and had been born of an ordinary earthly mother, and if He had not been preserved at the moment of His conception, He would have been as capable, as the other children of Adam, of committing all manner of crimes. This held Him in a state of profound humiliation. Beyond this He saw Himself charged with all the sins of the world as if they had been His own. *Peccata nostra sua esse voluit,* says St. Augustine, and He saw Himself obliged to bear before God the humiliation of a number of crimes as great as the drops of water and grains of sand in the sea.

O Jesus, who could understand all the humiliations Thou didst bear on earth to destroy my pride? How is it possible that after all this, my heart can tolerate for one single instant this frightful monster?

SECOND POINT

Hatred of the Heart of Jesus for the Glory and Esteem of the World

To know the second effect of humility in the Heart of our Redeemer, let us see His continual hatred for the esteem and glory of this world during the whole course of His life here below. He is the Only Son of God and is God equal to His Father. He is the King of glory, the sovereign Monarch of heaven and earth, who merits the homage and adoration of all creatures. If He were to display the palest ray of His majesty, the whole universe would fall prostrate at His feet to adore Him. But He permits none of His grandeur to appear, either at His birth or in the course of His life, not even after the Resurrection nor in the most adorable Sacrament where He is glorious and immortal. He fled when the Jews wished to make Him king, and declared that His kingdom is not of this world, so much did He detest the glory and honors of the world.

O Jesus, impress these sentiments upon my heart and grant that I may learn ever to esteem the praises of the world as poison from hell.

Love of the Heart of Jesus for Humiliation

Recall to your mind all the humiliations, all the confusion, contempt, abjection, opprobrium and ignominies that our most adorable Saviour bore in His Incarnation, in His Birth, in His Circumcision, in His Flight into Egypt, and in all the mysteries of His Passion. All these humiliations constitute a magnificent feast that His divine love has prepared and all the ignominies are as delicious viands, upon which He has feasted and satisfied His extreme hunger for abasement.

Whence did this insatiable hunger proceed, if not from His infinite love for His Heavenly Father and for us? This love gave Him the incredible desire to be humiliated and considered as nothing, to atone for the infinite injury and the inconceivable dishonor the sinner had shown to God. The sinner tears Him from His throne so that he may put himself in His Creator's place, preferring his own satisfactions to God's good pleasure, his own honor to that of God and his own will to the divine will. This injury only a God can perfectly repair by His own abasement.

That is why the incomprehensible love of the Son of God for His Father not only obliged Him to suffer so many humiliations, but also brought Him to the abyss of ignominies to seek his joys and delights, to repair more perfectly the dishonor shown to His Father. His love compelled Him also to deliver us from the eternal pains of hell, to acquire for us everlasting bliss in heaven, to destroy our pride, the source of all our sins, and to establish in our souls that humility which is the true foundation of all virtues.

Infinite thanks, O my Jesus, be to Thy holy humility. Everlasting praise to the Eternal Father who exalted Thee as highly as Thou hast been humiliated and has given Thee a name above all other names. May every knee in heaven, on earth and in hell bend to adore and glorify Jesus Christ and may every tongue confess my Saviour, rejoicing in the immense and eternal glory of His Father!

Ejaculatory prayer: Jesus, meek and humble of Heart, have mercy on us.

Jesu, mitis et humilis corde, miserere nobis.

EIGHTH MEDITATION

The Sacred Heart of Jesus Is the King of Martyrs

SUFFERINGS OF THE SACRED HEART OF JESUS BECAUSE OF OUR SINS

ALL THE SUFFERINGS of the holy martyrs pale into insignificance in comparison to the infinite sufferings of the adorable Heart of the King of martyrs. If you could number all the sins of the universe, you would count the myriad sharp arrows that pierced the divine Heart of our Saviour with so many wounds. These wounds caused the Sacred Heart to burn with love for His Eternal Father, whom He saw outraged and dishonored by innumerable crimes. O my Saviour, I hate all my sins, because they are the detestable executioners that brought Thy most gentle Heart to martrydom.

Again, picture to yourselves a countless number of miserable souls for whom our Saviour had an incredible love. He foresaw that, notwithstanding all His sufferings for their salvation, they would by their own fault be lost forever. This vision of the damned inflicted unutterable sorrow on the most charitable Heart of Jesus. O unhappy souls, why have you not loved Him, who has loved you more than Himself, since He has given His very life and blood for your salvation? O Dearest Jesus, give me all the hearts of these unfortunate souls, that I may love and praise Thee for them eternally.

SUFFERINGS OF THE SACRED HEART OF JESUS BECAUSE OF THE TRIALS AND TORMENTS OF THE MARTYRS AND CHRISTIANS

Recall to your minds all the sufferings, the agony, the trials and the torments of so many millions of martyrs and of all true Christians. All these afflictions are so many bleeding wounds for the most Sacred Heart of Jesus. His most benign Heart could suffer more than the tenderest of hearts because it was filled with an infinite charity for His beloved children. He had before His eyes all their crosses and sufferings. In the hour of affliction each one sought consolation from His adorable Heart. No human mind can understand the agonizing martyrdom suffered by this all paternal Heart in union with His heroic martyrs. This is expressed most remarkably in the words of the Prophet Isaias: *Vere dolores nostros ipse tulit,* [1] and also in the words of Saint Matthew: *Ipse nostras infirmitates accepit, et aegrotationes nostras portavit.* [2] Truly we can call the Sacred Heart the King of martyrs and the Glory of the Cross! How consoling it is for the afflicted to know that all their pain and sorrow have already been suffered by the most benign Heart of Jesus! He has borne all sufferings first out of love for His martyrs! Let us give ourselves also to Him to bear all our afflictions in union with immeasurable love with which He first suffered them.

SUFFERINGS OF THE SACRED HEART OF JESUS ON THE CROSS

All the other sufferings of our Saviour seem to diminish when compared to those borne by His divine Heart on the Cross. The

[1] Is. 53, 4.
[2] Matt. 8, 17.

sufferings of Calvary were so excruciating that the perfect body of our Saviour was broken with pain and sorrow, and His soul He commended into the hands of His Father. O my Saviour, what made Thee suffer so many torments, if it was not Thy infinite love for Thy Father and for us? Indeed, we can say that Thou hast died of loving sorrow and that Thy Heart has been torn and broken by sorrowing love for the glory of Thy Father and for our redemption. O most adorable Heart of Jesus, how shall I thank Thee for the excess of Thy bounty? Oh, that I could possess all the hearts of heaven and earth to sacrifice them in the flames of Thy love!

O Most Holy Father, how canst Thou refuse what anyone asks of Thee through the amiable Heart of Thy Son, broken with sorrow for love of Thee and for love of us? No, it is impossible. Rather wouldst Thou allow heaven and earth to disappear. It is, then, through this divine Heart overcome by love and sorrow for me that I implore Thee, O Adorable Father, to take full and entire possession of my heart and to establish there perfectly and forever the reign of the holy love of Jesus and Mary.

Ejaculatory prayer:

> Hail! Victim of all woes enthroned
> Upon the Cross, the Martyrs' King!
> Make Thou the Cross a joy intoned,
> The crown and glory that we sing.

> *Ave, dolorum victima,*
> *Centrum crucis, Rex Martyrum,*
> *Fac nostra sit Crux gloria,*
> *Amor, corona, gaudium.*

NINTH MEDITATION
The Sacred Heart of Jesus Is the Heart of Mary

FIRST POINT

MUTUAL LOVE OF THE SACRED HEARTS OF JESUS AND MARY

THE VIRGINAL HEART of the Blessed Mother of Jesus has more love for her Dear Son than all the angels and saints together; thus the Sacred Heart of the Only Son of Mary is so full of love for His most loving Mother that He is more to her than all created things together.

Let us offer to Jesus the Heart and love of His Blessed Mother in reparation for all our want of love and service towards Him. Let us offer to His most worthy Mother, who is also our Mother, the Heart and love of her Son in satisfaction for our ingratitude and infidelity towards her.

SECOND POINT

THE THREE DIVINE PERSONS GAVE THE HEART OF JESUS TO MARY, AND THROUGH HER TO US

Not only is the Blessed Virgin the first object, after God, of the ardent love of the Sacred Heart of Jesus, but the Sacred Heart is really the Heart of Mary for five principal reasons. The first three reasons are: 1. because the Eternal Father has given her the Heart of His Only-begotten Son as a father gives the heart of a son to his mother; 2. because the Son has given His most loving Heart to the most admirable of mothers; 3. because the Holy Ghost has given

Mary the very spirit of love which unites the Blessed Trinity in the Sacred Heart of her Son. These Three Divine Persons continually and eternally give Mary the adorable Heart of the God-Man, so that she may give us her most precious gift, the Sacred Heart of her Divine Son.

Incessant and everlasting praise be to the Father, to the Son, and to the Holy Ghost for this infinitely precious gift that They have given to our Blessed Mother and through her to us. O Most Holy Trinity, I offer Thee the most adorable Heart of Jesus and the most loving Heart of His Mother in thanksgiving for Thy infinite goodness in my regard. I also offer Thee, in union with those two most amiable Hearts, my own unworthy heart, with the hearts of all my brethren, humbly beseeching Thee to take full possession of them forever.

THIRD POINT

Other Reasons Why the Sacred Heart of Jesus Is the Holy Heart of Mary

The fourth reason why the Sacred Heart is truly the Heart of Mary is that the Eternal Father, having considered the Blessed Virgin from the very instant of her conception as the one chosen to be the Mother of God, gave her from the first moment of her life a love similar to His love for His Divine Son. According to many theologians, Mary had more love for Jesus at that moment than all the Seraphim will ever have. Therefore, Mary's incomparable love for Jesus drew Him into her sacred womb and into her Heart to rest there eternally as the Heart of her Heart and as a Divine Sun that sheds its celestial light into her soul and inflames it with divine fire.

The fifth reason why the Sacred Heart of Jesus is the heart of Mary is that, at the moment of the Incarnation, she cooperated with the Blessed Trinity to form the human Heart of Jesus, which was formed of her virginal blood. The blood of her holy Heart passed into the Heart of Jesus and received the perfection that was needed to form the Heart of the God-Man. This divinely human and humanly divine Heart dwelt in the sacred womb of Mary as a furnace of divine love, a furnace which transformed the Heart of Mary into the Heart of Jesus and made these two Hearts but one and the same Heart in a unity of spirit, affection and will.

The holy Heart of Mary was, therefore, always closely united to the Sacred Heart of her Divine Son. She always willed what He willed and also consented to act and to suffer so that the work of our salvation might be accomplished. Hence, the Fathers of the Church plainly assert that the Mother of the Saviour cooperated with Him in a very special way in the redemption of mankind. That is why our holy Redeemer told St. Bridget of Sweden, whose revelations have been approved by the Church, that He and His holy Mother worked in perfect harmony, *uno corde,* for our salvation.

Thus the Sacred Heart of Jesus is the Heart of Mary. These two Hearts are but one Heart, which was given to us by the Blessed Trinity and by our Blessed Mother, so that we, the children of Jesus and Mary, might have but one Heart with our Heavenly Father and our holy Mother and that we might love and glorify God with the same Heart, a Heart worthy of the infinite grandeur of His divine majesty.

Ejaculatory prayer: O Heart of Jesus and Mary, my most loving Heart!

O Cor Jesu et Mariae, Cor meum amantissimum!

Eight Other Meditations

ON THE SACRED HEART OF JESUS

FIRST MEDITATION
The Blessed Trinity Lives and Reigns in the Sacred Heart of Jesus

FIRST POINT

THE ETERNAL FATHER LIVES IN THE SACRED HEART OF JESUS

CONSIDER that the Eternal Father is in the Sacred Heart of Jesus, bringing to birth His Well-beloved Son and causing Him to live there the same all-holy and divine life that He lives in His own adorable bosom from all eternity. He imprints there a perfect image of His own divine Fatherhood, so that this humanly divine and divinely human Heart shall be Father to all the hearts of the children of God. Therefore, we should look upon Him, love and honor Him as our Loving Father, and endeavor to imprint upon our own hearts a perfect likeness of His life and virtues.

O Good Jesus, engrave the image of Thy most holy Heart upon our hearts and make us live only by love for Thy Heavenly Father. Would that we might die of love for Thee, as Thou didst die of love for Thy Eternal Father!

SECOND POINT

The Divine Word Lives and Reigns in the Sacred Heart of Jesus

Consider that the Eternal Word is in that royal Heart, united with it in the most intimate union imaginable, the hypostatic union, which causes that Heart to be worshipped with the adoration that is due to God. He is there with a life that is somehow more helpful, if one may so speak, than His life in the Heart and bosom of His Father. The Word lives but does not rule in the Heart and bosom of the Heavenly Father; whereas He lives and rules in the Heart of the God-Man, ruling over all human passions which are centered in the heart so absolutely that they do not stir except by His order.

O Jesus, King of my heart, live and rule over my passions, uniting them with Thine, never allowing them to be used except under Thy guidance and for Thy glory alone!

THIRD POINT

The Holy Ghost Lives and Reigns in the Sacred Heart of Jesus

Consider that the Holy Ghost lives and reigns ineffably in the Heart of Jesus, where He conceals the infinite treasures of the knowledge and the wisdom of God. He fills the Sacred Heart with all His gifts to a pre-eminent degree, according to His divine words: *Et requiescet super eum Spiritus Domini, Spiritus sapientiae et intellectus, Spiritus consilii et fortitudinis, Spiritus scientiae et pietatis, et replebit eum Spiritus timoris Domini.*[1]

Consider, finally, that these Three Divine Persons live and reign in the Heart of the Saviour, as if they were seated on the most high

[1] Isa. 11, 2-3.

throne of their love, in the primal heaven of their glory, in the paradise of their dearest delights. They there shed abroad, with inexplicable abundance and profusion, wonderful lights, and the burning fires and flames of their eternal love.

O Most Holy Trinity, infinite praise be to Thee forever for all the wonders of love that Thou dost work in the Heart of my Jesus! I offer Thee my heart, with the hearts of all my brethren, begging Thee most humbly to take entire possession of them, to destroy in them everything displeasing to Thee, and to establish there the sovereign rule of Thy divine love.

Ejaculatory Prayer: O Most Holy Trinity, eternal life of Hearts, reign in all hearts forever. *O sacrosancta Trinitas, aeterna vita cordium, in corde regnes omnium!*

SECOND MEDITATION

The Sacred Heart of Jesus Is the Sanctuary and the Image of the Divine Perfections

FIRST POINT

THE DIVINE PERFECTIONS SUBSIST AND REIGN IN THE SACRED HEART OF JESUS

LET US ADORE and contemplate all the perfections of the divine nature, subsisting and reigning in the Sacred Heart of Jesus: that is to say, the eternity of God, the infinity of God, His love, charity, justice, mercy, power, immortality, wisdom, goodness, glory, felicity, patience, holiness and all other perfections.

Let us adore these divine perfections in all the wonderful effects they produce in the divine Heart of the Son of God. Let us give wholehearted thanks for these manifestations, and offer them all the worship, glory and love which have been and shall be rendered to them eternally by that same Heart.

SECOND POINT

THE DIVINE PERFECTIONS STAMP THEIR ETERNAL IMPRESS ON THE SACRED HEART OF JESUS

Let us consider that those adorable perfections imprint their image and likeness on the divine Heart of Our Lord, in a manner infinitely more excellent than all human and angelic minds can conceive or express. The adorable Heart of Jesus bears within itself the image of eternity by its perfect detachment forever from things fleeting and temporal and by its exceeding great affection for things divine and eternal. It bears the image of immortality by Its infinite love for the Heavenly Father and for us, a love whose immensity reaches everywhere, in heaven, on earth and under the earth. If we consider the nature of that incomparable Heart, we shall see without difficulty that it bears within itself a living likeness of all the other perfections of the Godhead.

O wonderful Heart of Jesus, we offer Thee our hearts; impress upon them, we beseech Thee, some reflection of that divine likeness, so that in us may be accomplished the commandment of our divine Master: *Estote perfecti, sicut Pater vester caelestis perfectus est.*[1]

THIRD POINT

The Divine Mercy Should be the Object of Our Very Special Devotion

Of all the divine perfections mirrored in the Sacred Heart of our Saviour we should have a very special devotion to divine mercy and we should endeavor to engrave its image on our heart. To this end three things must be done. The first is to pardon with all our heart and promptly forget the offenses done us by our neighbor. The second is to have compassion on his bodily sufferings, and to relieve and succor him. The third is to compassionate the spiritual misfortunes of our brethren, which are much more deserving of commiseration than the corporal ills. For this reason we ought to have great pity on the numbers of wretched souls who have no pity on themselves, using our prayers, our example and our teaching to safeguard them from the eternal torments of hell.

O most gracious and merciful Heart of Jesus, imprint on our hearts a perfect image of Thy great perfections, so that we may ful-

[1] Matt. 5, 48.

fil the commandment Thou hast given us: *Estote misericordes, sicut Pater vester caelestis misericors est.*[2]

Ejaculatory Prayer: O Holy God, O Strong God, O Immortal God, have mercy on us. *Sanctus Deus, sanctus fortis, sanctus immortalis, miserere nobis!*

[2] Luke 6, 36.

THIRD MEDITATION

The Sacred Heart of Jesus Is the Temple, the Altar and the Censer of Divine Love

THE SACRED HEART OF JESUS IS THE TEMPLE OF DIVINE LOVE

THE HOLY GHOST, love uncreated and eternal, built this magnificent temple and fashioned it of the virginal blood of the Mother of love. It is dedicated to eternal love. It is infinitely more sacred, more noble and more venerable than all the temples material and spiritual in heaven and on earth. In this temple God receives worship, praise, and glory worthy of His infinite greatness. In this temple the supreme Preacher continually teaches us most eloquently. It is an everlasting temple that shall have no end. It is the center of all holiness, incapable of any profanation. It is adorned with all the Christian virtues in the highest degree, and with all the perfections of the divine nature, as with so many living images of the Eternal Godhead.

Let us rejoice in the vision of all the splendors of this wonderful temple and all the glories there rendered to the divine majesty.

SECOND POINT

THE SACRED HEART OF JESUS AN ALTAR OF DIVINE LOVE

The Heart of Jesus is not only the temple, but it is also the altar of divine love. On that altar the sacred flame of omnipotent love burns night and day. On that altar the great High Priest Jesus continually offers to the Most Holy Trinity manifold sacrifices and supreme oblation.

First, He offers Himself as a sacrifice and victim of love, the most holy and precious victim that ever was or can be. He sacrifices utterly and entirely His body, His blood, His soul, His whole life, all His thoughts, all His words, all His actions and all that He suffered on earth. Moreover, He makes that sacrifice perpetually, with a love that is boundless and infinite.

Secondly, He sacrifices everything the Heavenly Father has given Him, namely, all rational and irrational creatures, animate and inaminate beings, which he immolates as so many victims in praise of His Father; but, above all, He sacrifices human beings, the good and the wicked, the blessed and the reprobate. The good He offers as victims of love to His divine goodness. The evil He immolates as victims of the wrath of God, to His awful justice: *Omnis victima salietur.*[1] Thus the great High Priest sacrifices all things to the glory of His Father on the altar of His Heart. Therefore, He alone may rightly say: *Laetus obtuli universa.*[2]

Let us offer ourselves to Him and beg Him to rank us with the victims of His love, to consume us as holocausts in the divine flames burning incessantly on the altar of His Sacred Heart.

THIRD POINT

The Sacred Heart of Jesus is a Censer of Divine Love

The Sacred Heart of Jesus is not only the temple and the altar, but also the censer of divine love. It is the golden thurible described in the eighth chapter of the Apocalypse, which St. Augustine interprets as the loving Heart of Jesus. In that precious censer all the worship, praise, prayers, desires and affections of all the saints are

[1] Mark 9, 48.
[2] 1 Para. 29, 17.

placed, like so many grains of incense to be offered to God in the Heart of His Well-beloved Son, ascending as a most pleasing odor to His divine majesty. There we also must place all our prayers, all our desires, all our devotions, and all the pious affections of our hearts, yes, our very hearts themselves, with all that we do and all that we are, beseeching the King of all hearts to purify and sanctify all these things and to offer them to His Father as a heavenly incense of sweet fragrance.

Thus the Sacred Heart of our Jesus is the temple, the altar, the censer, the priest, the victim of divine love, all for our sake, performing on our behalf the functions of those divine offices. O love so abundant! O my Saviour, how wonderful are Thy loving kindnesses! Ah, what reverence and praise I should give to Thy loving Heart in return! O most blessed Heart of my Jesus, let me be naught but heart and love towards Thee and let all hearts on heaven and earth be immolated to Thy praise and glory!

Ejaculatory Prayer:

> Hail, priest of hearts and victim, hail!
> Alone Thou equal art to God.
> Most worthy Temple, Holy Grail,
> And Altar, holiest to laud.

> *Ave, Sacerdos cordium,*
> *Ave, Deo par Victima,*
> *Templum Deo dignissimum,*
> *Et Ara sacratissima.*

FOURTH MEDITATION

The Sacred Heart of Jesus Loves Us with an Everlasting and a Boundless Love

THE SACRED HEART OF JESUS LOVES US WITH AN EVERLASTING LOVE

THE DIVINE HEART of our Saviour is filled with eternal love for us. To realize this truth one should understand two things about eternity: first, that it has neither beginning nor end; secondly, that it comprises in itself all ages, past, present and future, all the years, months, weeks, days, hours and moments of the past, present and future, and that it comprises them in a fixed and permanent manner, holding all those things united and joined together in one indivisible point. That is how eternity differs from time. Time runs on incessantly; as one moment arrives, another elapses and is left behind, and so one never sees two moments of time together. But in eternity everything is permanent; whatever is eternal always remains of the same extension.

That is why the eternal love of the Sacred Heart of Jesus for us comprises two elements. First, this incomparable Heart has loved us from all eternity, before we were and could have known and loved it, even in spite of the vision and knowledge that it had of all our offenses which were present to its vision as they are now. Secondly, the amiable Heart of Jesus loves us at every moment with all the love wherewith it has ever loved us and shall love us throughout all eternity. Thus we can see the difference between God's love and ours. Our love is a passing act; the love of God is constant. The love that

God has exercised towards us for a hundred thousand years remains in His Heart together with that which He will dispense a hundred thousand years from now. Eternity implies that in God there is nothing past nor future, but all is present, so that God loves us now with all the love wherewith He has loved us from all eternity and wherewith He will love us forever.

O eternity of love! O eternal love! If I had existed from all eternity, I should have been bound to love Thee from all eternity; and yet, my God, I have not begun to love Thee as I should. But at least let me begin now, O my Saviour, to love Thee as Thou wouldst be loved. O God of my heart, I give myself to Thee to be united to Thy ceaseless love for me from all eternity. I surrender myself to Thee to be united to the love wherewith Thou lovest Thy Father before all centuries, so as to love the Father and the Son with an eternal love.

SECOND POINT

The Sacred Heart of Jesus Loves Us with a Boundless Love

The loving Heart of Jesus loves us with a boundless love. The divine and uncreated love which possesses that adorable Heart, is nothing else but God Himself. Now, since God is unlimited, His love is also unlimited. Since God is everywhere, His love is everywhere, in all places and in all things. Therefore, the Sacred Heart of Jesus loves us not only in heaven, but He also loves us on earth. He loves us in the sun, in the stars and in all created things. He loves us in the hearts of all the denizens of heaven and in the hearts of all persons that have some measure of charity for us on earth. All love for ourselves existing in the hearts in heaven and on earth is a participation in the love of the Sacred Heart of Jesus. Moreover, He loves us even in the hearts of our enemies despite the hatred they bear us. I even make bold to say that He loves us in hell, in the hearts of the devils and the damned, in spite of all their wrath and hatred, since the divine love is everywhere, filling heaven and earth like the presence of God.

O boundless love, I plunge myself into thy fires and flames that fill all created beings, in order to love my God and my Saviour in all places and in all things. O Jesus, I offer Thee all the boundless love of Thy Heart, of the adorable Heart of Thy Divine Father, the lovable heart of Thy holy Mother, and of all the hearts that love Thee in heaven and on earth. I ardently desire that all creatures of the universe be transformed into flaming fires of love towards Thee.

Ejaculatory Prayer: How late have I loved Thee, O goodness so ancient and yet so new, how late have I loved Thee. *Sero te amavi, bonitas tam antiqua et tam nova, sero te amavi.*

FIFTH MEDITATION

The Sacred Heart of Jesus Is the Source of the Life of the God-Man, of the Mother of God, and of the Children of God

THE SACRED HEART OF JESUS IS THE SOURCE OF THE LIFE OF THE GOD-MAN

THE ADORABLE HEART of our Saviour is the source of the life of the God-Man, and consequently is the source of all the thoughts and feelings of the Son of God on earth, of all the words He pronounced, of all the actions He performed, of all the sufferings He endured, and of the incomprehensible love wherewith He did and suffered all things for our salvation. Therefore, it is to Thy loving Heart, O my Jesus, that our obligation is due. What shall we do to thank Thee? We can do nothing more pleasing to Thee than to offer Thee thy most divine Heart. I offer it then to Thee, my Saviour, in union with the infinite love wherewith it hath accomplished so many wonderful things for our Redemption.

THE SACRED HEART OF JESUS IS THE SOURCE OF THE LIFE OF THE MOTHER OF GOD

The Sacred Heart of Jesus is the source of the life of Mary, the Mother of God. When that admirable Mother was carrying her Beloved Son in her blessed womb, her virginal Heart was the source of the natural bodily life of her divine Child, but the Heart of that adorable Child was, at the same time, the source of the spiritual and supernatural life of His most worthy Mother. Hence the divine Heart of the Only Son of Mary was the source of all the pious thoughts and feelings of His Blessed Mother, of all the sacred words she spoke, of all the good deeds she performed, of all the virtues she practised, and of all the pains and sorrows she suffered in order to cooperate with her Beloved Son in the work of our Salvation.

Praise eternal, O my Jesus, to Thy divine Heart! O my Redeemer, in thanksgiving for the great wonders of grace that Thy filial Heart hath wrought in Thy glorious Mother, I offer her maternal Heart flaming with love for Thee.

THIRD POINT

The Sacred Heart of Jesus is the Source of Life of the Children of God

The Sacred Heart of Jesus is the source of life of all the children of God. Since it is the source of the life of the Head, it is also the source of life of the members; and since it is the source of life of the Father and the Mother, it is the source of life of the children. That is why we should regard and honor that benign Heart as the source and origin of all the good thoughts in the minds of all Christians, of all the holy words that have issued from their lips, of all the virtues that they have practised and of all the toil they have borne for their sanctification as Christians.

O my Saviour, may all these things be transmuted into immortal praise to Thy most Sacred Heart! O Jesus, since Thou hast given me that very Heart to be the source of my life, let it be, I beseech Thee, the sole source of all my feelings and affections, of all the faculties and functions of my soul, and of all the use I make of my interior and exterior senses! In fine, let it be the soul of my soul, the spirit of my spirit, and the Heart of my heart!

Ejaculatory Prayer: O Heart of Jesus, principle of all good, to Thee be praise and glory for ever.
   O Cor Jesu, Principium omnium bonorum, tibi laus, tibi gloria in aeternum!

SIXTH MEDITATION
The Three Hearts of Jesus Which Are But One Heart

The Divine Heart of Jesus

WE HAVE THREE HEARTS to adore in our Saviour which, nevertheless, are but one single Heart by virtue of the hypostatic union.

The first is His divine Heart existing from all eternity in the bosom of His Adorable Father, which is but one Heart and one love with the love and Heart of His Father, and which, with the Heart and love of His Father, is the source of the Holy Spirit. Therefore, when He gave us His Heart, He also gave us the Heart of His Father and of His Adorable Spirit; hence His marvelous words: *Sicut dilexit me Pater, et ego dilexi vos.* "I love you with the same Heart and the same love wherewith I love my Father." [1] My Father loves me with an eternal, boundless and infinite love; I love you also with a love that is eternal, boundless and infinite. My Father causes Me to be what I am, God like to Himself and Only Son of God; and I make you to be by grace and participation what I am by nature and essence, that is to say, Gods and children of God, seeing that you have but One and the Same Father as I, a Father who loves you with the same Heart and the same love wherewith He loves me: *Dilexisti eos sicut et me dilexisti.* [2] My Eternal Father has constituted Me universal heir of all His goods: *Constituit haeredem universorum;* [3] and I make you My co-heirs: *Haeredes Dei et cohae-*

[1] John 15, 9.
[2] John 17, 23.
[3] Heb. 1, 2.

126

redes Christi;[4] I promise to give you possession of all My treasures: *Super omnia bona sua constituet eum.*[5] My Father finds all His pleasure and delight in Me; and I take My delight and pleasure in you: *Deliciae meae esse cum filiis hominum.*[6]

O goodness! O love! O God of love, how is it possible for the hearts of men to be so hard and cold towards Thee who art all aflame with the fire of love towards them? Oh, let all my joy and delight be in thinking of Thee, in speaking of Thee, in serving and loving Thee! O my All, let me be wholly Thine, and do Thou alone possess all that is in me.

SECOND POINT

The Spiritual Heart of Jesus

The second Heart of Jesus is His spiritual Heart, which is the will of His holy soul, a purely spiritual faculty, whose function is to love what is lovable and to hate what is hateful. But the divine Saviour so perfectly sacrificed His human will to His Divine Father that He never exercised it while on earth and will never exercise it even in heaven, but He sought uniquely and solely His Father's will, according to those words of His: "I seek not my own will, but the will of him that sent me."[7] "I came down from heaven, not to do my own will but the will of Him that sent me."[8] Now, it is out of love for us that Our Lord renounced His own will, in order to perform the work of our salvation solely by the will of His Father, in particular when He prayed to Him in the Garden of Olives: *Pater, non mea voluntas, sed tua fiat,* "Father, not my will but thine be done!"[9]

---

[4] Rom. 8, 17.
[5] Matt. 24, 47.
[6] Prov. 8, 31.
[7] John 5, 30.
[8] John 6, 38.
[9] Luke 22, 42.

O God of my heart, if for love of me Thou didst sacrifice Thy utterly holy and divine will, how much more should I renounce my own will for love of Thee, wholly depraved and corrupted as it is by sin! Ah, let me renounce it with all my heart forever, imploring Thee most humbly, O my adorable Redeemer, to crush it like a serpent full of venom and to establish in its place the rule of Thy divine will.

THIRD POINT

THE CORPOREAL HEART OF JESUS

The third Heart of Jesus is the Sacred Heart of His deified body, a furnace of love divine and of incomparable love for us. Since the corporeal Heart is hypostatically united to the Person of the Word, It is enkindled with flames of infinite love for us. Its love is so intense that it constrains the Son of God to bear us continually in His Heart; to fix His eyes ever upon us; to take such a great interest in the smallest things concerning us that He verily numbers all the hairs of our head, allowing not one of them to perish; to ask His Father that we might make our eternal abode within His bosom: *Pater, quos dedisti mihi, volo ut ubi sum ego; et illi sint mecum;*[10] and to assure us that, if we vanquish the enemies of His glory and of our salvation, He will make us sit with Him on His own throne, and will let us enter into possession of the same kingdom and the same glory that His Eternal Father has given Him.

Oh, how abundant and rapturous is the love of Jesus for such faithless and ungrateful men as we! O Jesus, my love, either take away my life or let me live only to love Thee, to praise and glorify Thee unceasingly. Let me die a thousand deaths rather than willingly do anything to grieve Thee! Thou hast three Hearts which are but one and the same Heart, a Heart wholly devoted to loving me continually. Would that I possessed all the hearts in the universe that I might consume them in Thy holy love!

[10] John 17, 24.

Ejaculatory Prayer: I love Thee, O Most Loving Jesus, I love Thee, O infinite goodness, I love Thee with my whole heart and I wish to love Thee more and more.

Amo te, amantissime Jesu, amo te, bonitas infinita, amo te ex toto corde meo, et magis atque magis amare volo.

SEVENTH MEDITATION
The Miracles of the Sacred Heart of Jesus

FIRST POINT

MIRACLES OF THE SACRED HEART OF JESUS IN THE REALM OF NATURE

SET BEFORE YOUR EYES the realm of nature, the great universe comprising so many wonderful things, namely, the heavens, the sun, the moon, the stars and comets, the four elements, of which the air is peopled by such a great variety of birds; the earth, replete with its marvelous abundance of animals, trees, plants, flowers, fruits, metals, stones; the sea, filled with such a prodigious multitude of fishes. Add to that the creatures of reason, men and angels; consider them in the natural state of their creation. What a miracle to have made this amazing universe out of nothing! It is not a miracle, it is a world of miracles without number. Count all the creatures made by God and you will count so many miracles that God has performed in drawing them from the abyss of nothingness. Number all the moments that have elapsed since the creation of the world and you will number so many miracles, since preservation is a continuous creation. There is also an infinite number of other wonders perpetually wrought in the governance of this universe. Now, who is the author of those innumerable miracles? It is the inconceivable goodness and the incomprehensible love of the divine Heart of that adorable Word, mentioned by St. John the Evangelist in the first words of his Gospel: *Omnia per ipsum facta sunt.* It is because of His love for us that He has made all things, even though He had always before His eyes the ingratitudes, the offenses and the crimes without limit which He was obliged to suffer and still endures every day from us.

That is why all those things which He created are so many tongues and voices preaching to us unceasingly the ineffable charity of His most gracious Heart and exhorting us to adore Him, to love Him and to glorify Him in every possible manner.

Heaven and earth, says St. Augustine, and all things contained therein, cease not to tell me that I should love my God: *Caelum et terra et omnia quae in eis sunt, non cessant mihi dicere ut amem Deum meum.*

SECOND POINT

MIRACLES OF THE SACRED HEART OF JESUS IN THE REALM OF GRACE

Picture the realm of grace, which comprises an infinitude of wonders incomparably surpassing those of the world of nature. It contains all the miracles of sanctity that have been wrought on the earth by the Holy of holies; all the wonders that transpired in the Mother of grace; the entire Church Militant; all the Sacraments, with all the marvelous effects which they produce; all the wonderful things that divine grace has effected and will effect in the lives of all the saints that have been and that shall be in this world. What is the source of all those wonders? Is it not the inconceivable charity of the blessed Heart of our Redeemer, who has established and constantly preserves this amazing world of grace on earth, for love of us?

O my Jesus, let all these wonders of Thy most loving Heart and all the powers of Thy divinity and Thy humanity be employed to bless Thee and praise Thee unceasingly and eternally: *Benedicite omnes virtutes Domini Domino.*[1]

[1] Dan. 3, 61.

Miracles of the Sacred Heart of Jesus in the Realm of Glory

Raise your mind and your heart to heaven, to contemplate the realm of glory, the fair, great and glorious city of Heaven, of which all the citizens are forever freed from all kinds of tribulations and showered with countless blessings. Behold that innumerable army of the blessed, *quam nemo dinumerae poterat*[2] who are more dazzling than the sun, who possess incalculable riches, joys unspeakable, and glories indescribable. Consider the inconceivable happiness which awaits you in that heavenly Jerusalem, since the Holy Ghost declares that never has eye seen, nor ear heard, nor human heart understood nor can ever understand the infinite treasures that God has prepared there for them that love Him. Now, what has made heaven and who is the author of all the miracles contained therein? It is the intense love of the Sacred Heart of the Son of God, who has merited it by His blood, who has filled it with an ocean of unutterable delights, to give us the full and perfect possession of it eternally.

O my Saviour, graciously let me offer Thee, I beg Thee, as an act of thanksgiving, all the glories and wonders of paradise! If I were possessed of a hundred thousand paradises, how gladly would I, by the help of Thy grace, divest myself of them so as to sacrifice them to Thy eternal praise!

Ejaculatory Prayer: Let the mercies of the Lord give glory to him: and his wonderful works to the children of man.

Confiteantur Domino misericordiae ejus, et mirablilia ejus filiis hominum.

[2] Apoc. 7, 9.

EIGHTH MEDITATION

The Sacred Heart of Jesus Is a Furnace of Love, Purifying, Illuminating, Sanctifying, Transforming and Deifying

FIRST POINT

THE SACRED HEART OF JESUS A FURNACE OF LOVE FOR US

THE MOST LOVING HEART of our benign Saviour is a burning furnace of most pure love for us; a furnace of purifying love, of illuminating love, of sanctifying love, of transforming love, and of deifying love. His love is a purifying love, in which the hearts of holy souls are purified more perfectly than gold in the furnace; an illuminating love, which scatters the darkness of hell with which the earth is covered and lets us into the wonderful brilliance of heaven; *de tenebris vos vocavit in admirabile lumen suum;*[1] a sanctifying love, which destroys sin in our souls in order to establish there the kingdom of grace; a transforming love, which transforms serpents into doves, wolves into lambs, beasts into angels, children of the devil into children of God, children of wrath and malediction into children of grace and blessing; a deifying love, which makes gods of men, *ego dixi dii estis,* letting them share in the holiness of God, His mercy, His patience, His goodness, His love, His charity and His other divine perfections: *Divinae consortes naturae.*[2]

O divine love of my Jesus, I give myself wholly to Thee; purify me, enlighten me, sanctify me, transform me into Thee, that I may be naught but love for my God.

[1] 1 Pet. 2, 9.
[2] 2 Pet. 1, 4.

SECOND POINT

The Furnace of the Sacred Heart of Jesus Radiates Love to all Beings

The august Heart of Jesus is a furnace of love which spreads its fiery flames in all directions, in heaven, on earth, and throughout the whole universe. Its fiery flames would have consumed the hearts of the Seraphim and would have enkindled all the hearts of earth, if the terrible chill of sin had not set in. Those divine fires transform all the hearts of heavenly lovers into so many furnaces of love for Him who is all love for them.

All creatures on earth, even those which are senseless, inanimate and irrational, feel the effects of the incredible goodness of that magnificent Heart, since He loves all things that are and hates nothing that He has made, sin being the only thing that He did not make, the only object of His hatred: *Diligis omnia quae sunt, et nihil odisti eorum quae fecisti.*[3]

Jesus has an extraordinary love for men, as well for the good as the wicked, for His friends as for His enemies, for whom He has such intense charity that even the overwhelming torrents and floods of their innumerable sins are not able to extinguish it: *Aquae multae non potuerunt extinguere charitatem.*[4] Not a moment elapses that He does not grant them manifold natural and supernatural favors, corporal and spiritual, even while they are offending Him and dishonoring Him by their misdeeds.

The divine fires of the precious Heart of the Son of God reach even into hell, to the devils and the damned, preserving their being, life, and the natural perfections which He gave them at creation and not punishing them as much as they have deserved for their sins, for which His divine justice might very justly chastise them much more severely than it does: *Non est qui se abscondat a calore ejus.*[5]

[3] Wisdom 11, 25.
[4] Cant. 8, 7.
[5] Ps. 18, 7.

O sacred fires and flames of the Heart of my Saviour, rush in upon my heart and the hearts of all my brethren, and kindle them into as many furnaces of love for my Most Loving Jesus!

THIRD POINT

INTENSITY OF THE LOVE OF THE SACRED HEART OF JESUS

Imagine all the charity, all the affections, all the tender and intimate feelings of all the hearts that the omnipotent hand of God might fashion as being collected and united in one heart large enough to contain them. Would they not all be capable of forming one unimaginable furnace of love? But realize that all the fires and flames of such a furnace would not make one tiny spark of the immense love with which the infinitely loving Heart of Jesus is inflamed towards you, O Christian soul.

O furnace infinitely to be desired! Who will grant me to be plunged into that burning fire? O Mother of Jesus, O all ye angels, O all ye holy saints of Jesus, I give myself to you all and to each in particular, and I give you also all my brothers and sisters in Christ, and all the inhabitants of earth, that you may cast us all into the abyss of that sacred furnace! Attend and hear, O vast furnace of love! A tiny straw asks most humbly and earnestly to be plunged, buried, lost, devoured and consumed wholly in thy sacred flames and thy holy fires forever and ever!

Ejaculatory Prayer: O fire which ever burnest and is never extinguished. O love which is ever fervent and never grows tepid, inflame me wholly that I may love Thee wholly.

O ignis qui semper ardes et nunquam extingueris. O amor qui semper ferves et nunquam tepescis, accende me totum, ut totus diligam te!

MASS
AND OFFICE OF
THE SACRED HEART OF JESUS

On July 29, 1672, St. John Eudes addressed a circular letter to his spiritual children, the Priests of the Congregation of Jesus and Mary and the Religious of Our Lady of Charity, enjoining them to celebrate a solemn feast in honor of the Sacred Heart of Jesus on October 20. He sent them for this occasion a special Office and Mass, which he had composed two years before. Both these liturgical documents had been previously approved by the Archbishop of Rouen and by the Bishops of Rennes, Evreux, Bayeux and Lisieux. The Saint was authorized to celebrate the Feast of the Sacred Heart in the houses of his Orders as a double of the first class with octave. The use of the Office and Mass was also permitted on the first Thursday of the month, unless it was hindered by an office of nine lessons.

The Office of the Sacred Heart is a complete office with lessons for the eight days of the octave. Invivatory, hymns, antiphons, versicles, lessons, responsaries and collect—everything is proper in this office as in that of the great feasts of the Church. Only the Office of the Feast Day with its English translation is included in this edition. The Latin hymns were composed by St. John Eudes and the other parts were borrowed from Sacred Scripture and from the Fathers of the Church. By combining and adapting them to the devotion to the Sacred Heart, the Saint was able to endow his office with a definite personal character and make it at once highly original and most unified. The dominant thought is that which Our Lord develops in the discourse after the Last Supper, when He reminds His Apostles of the love He has never ceased to show them and exhorts them to abide in His love.

The Mass brings out the same thought as the Office. The Sequence, an imitation of the *Lauda Sion*, is noteworthy. The author here celebrates, with transports of joy and love, the glories of the Sacred Heart. The depth of thought, the exuberance of feeling, and the perfection of form make it a real masterpiece. Writers who have dealt with both the Office and the Mass are unanimous in their praise.

"These offices," said Cardinal Satolli in speaking of the two Offices of the Sacred Hearts composed by St. John Eudes, "are marked by such sweet and intense piety that only the heart of a saint can devise such forms."[1]

In his book on *La Mère de Saumaise,* Father de Curley, S.J., examines the Mass of St. John Eudes. "If we had to give a name to this Mass," he says, "we shall call it the *Mass of Fire*. It is eternal love breaking forth in notes of affectionate supplication."[2]

After studying this Office and Mass, Father Bainvel writes: "In them we have, indeed, an original work that in parts, by the harmonious blending of its wealth of profound thought, of poetic rapture, of unction and solid piety, all inspired by the Scriptures and the Fathers, recalls the admirable Office of the Blessed Sacrament. With regard to the general sentiments, these breathe the most perfect spirit of devotion to the Sacred Heart, especially the spirit of love, the love of man who would respond to the love of God. . . . The Mass is wholly a Mass of love, wholly filled with the Sacred Heart of Jesus, with His love for God and for us, with our love for Him. It is indeed a sublime and beautiful liturgical work, by means of which Fr. Eudes' influence was extended to the societies most deeply imbued with the spirit of the devotion of Paray, and will continue to be felt therein."[3]

After the establishment of the Feast of the Sacred Heart in the Eudistic Orders in 1672, it was adopted by other religious Congregations, notably the Benedictine Nuns of Montmartre, the Benedictine Nuns of the Blessed Sacrament, and the Religious of Our Lady of Corbeil. The Office and Mass used by these communities were those

[1] Quoted by Rev. A. LeDoré in his *Circular*, January 6, 1909, p. 6.

[2] Quoted by Lebrun in *Le B. Jean Eudes et le Culte du Coeur de Jésus* (Paris, 1917), p. 39.

[3] Bainvel, *Devotion to the Sacred Heart* (London, 1924), p. 269-277.

of St. John Eudes. Even in many convents of the Visitation Order, after the miraculous apparitions of Paray-le-Monial, the liturgical works of St. John Eudes were in use until 1750.[4]

The Eudist Fathers and the Religious of Our Lady of Charity of the Refuge and of the Good Shepherd continue to our day to celebrate the Feast of the Sacred Heart on October 20, with the Office and Mass of their Founder. Only when, in consequence of the vigorous liturgical campaign of Dom Gueranger, it was declared that the Bishops had no right to authorize new feasts and offices in their dioceses and that the authorizations granted by them were null and void, did the Eudist Orders have recourse to the Holy See for a special approval. On December 12, 1861, the Congregation of Rites authorized them to preserve the Feasts of the Sacred Heart of Jesus and of the Holy Heart of Mary established by their Founder, and to celebrate them with the Mass and Office composed by him.

[4] Lebrun, *op. cit.*, p. 142 *et seq.*

MASS OF THE SACRED HEART OF JESUS

October 20

Introit

Gaudeamus omnes in Domino diem festum celebrantes in honorem Cordis amantissimi Redemptoris nostri Jesu Christi, cujus amorem adorant Seraphim psallentes in unum: Ecce cujus imperium manet in æternum. *Ps.* 110. Confitebor tibi, Domine, in toto corde meo in consilio justorum et congregatione, Gloria Patri. Gaudeamus.

Introit

Let us rejoice in the Lord, while celebrating this Festival in honor of the Most Loving Heart of our Redeemer, Jesus Christ, whose love the Seraphim adore with one harmonious chant. Lo! His Kingdom is established forever. Ps. 110. I will praise thee, O Lord, with my whole heart; in the council of the just, and in the congregation. Glory.

Oratio

Pater misericordiarum, et Deus totius consolationis, qui propter nimiam charitatem qua dilexisti nos, dilectissimi Filii tui Cor amantissimum nobis ineffabili bonitate donasti, ut te uno corde cum ipso perfecte diligamus; præsta, quæsumus, ut cordibus nostris inter se et cum Corde Jesu in unum consummatis, onmia nostra in humilitate et caritate ejus fiant, atque, ipso interveniente, justa cordis nostri desideria compleantur. Per eumdum Dominum.

Collect

O Father of mercies and God of all consolation, who by the exceeding love with which Thou hast loved us, hast given us with ineffable goodness, the Heart of Thy Beloved Son, so that having but one heart with Him, we may love Thee perfectly; grant, we beseech Thee, that our hearts, being consumed in unity among themselves and with the Heart of Jesus, we may perform all our works in His humility and charity and that by His mediation the just desires of our hearts may be accomplished. Through the same Lord.

Lectio Ezechielis Prophetae (c. 36)

Haec dicit Dominus Deus: Sanctificavi nomen meum magnum, ut

Lesson from the Prophet Ezechiel (c. 36)

Thus saith the Lord God: I will sanctify my great name that the

sciant gentes quia ego Dominus, ait Dominus exercituum, cum sanctificatus fuero in vobis coram eis. Tollam quippe vos de gentibus et congregabo vos de universis terris et adducam vos in terram vestram. Et effundam super vos aquam mundam, et mundabimini ab omnibus inquinamentis vestris et ab universis idolis vestris mundabo vos. Cor novum et spiritum novum ponam in medio vestri. Et auferam cor lapideum de carne vestra, et dabo vobis cor carneum; et Spiritum meum ponam in medio vestri.

Gentiles may know that I am the Lord, saith the Lord of hosts, when I shall be sanctified in you before their eyes. For I will take you from among the Gentiles and will gather you together out of all the countries and will bring you into your own land. And I will pour upon you clean water and you shall be cleansed from all your filthiness; and I will cleanse you from all your idols. And I will give you a new heart and a new spirit within you: and I will take away the stony heart out of your flesh and will give you a heart of flesh. And I will put my spirit in the midst of you.

Graduale (Gal. 4; Phil. 2; Eph. 5)

Quoniam estis filii Dei, misit Deus Spiritum et Cor Filii sui in corda vestra clamantem: Abba Pater. Hoc sentite in cordibus vestris quod et in corde ipsius: et ambulate in dilectione, sicut et ipse dilexit nos.

V. (Joan. 15) Sicut dilexit me Pater, et ego dilexi vos: et hoc est praeceptum meum, ut diligatis invicem, sicut dilexi vos. Manete ergo in dilectione mea.

Gradual (Gal. 5; Phil. 2; Eph. 5)

And because you are sons of God, God hath sent the Spirit and Heart of His Son into your hearts, crying: Abba, Father. Have in your hearts the sentiments of His Heart; and walk in love, as Christ also hath loved us.

V. (John 15) As the Father hath loved me, I also have loved you: and this is my commandment, that you love one another, as I have loved you. Abide in my love.

Alleluia. V. (Ps. 56; 2 Mach.)

Paratum Cor meum, Deus Cordis mei, paratum Cor meum, ut quæ placita sunt tibi faciam semper, corde magno et animo volenti.

Alleluia (Ps. 56; 2. Mach.)

My heart is ready, O God, my heart is ready to do all that thou willest, with a generous heart and resolute will.

Sequentia

Gaudeamus exultantes,
Cordis Jesu personantes
Divina præcordia.

Sequence

Exultations joyfully upraising
Songs the Heart of Jesus praising,
In jubilant ecstasy.

Hæc est dies veneranda,
In qua Patris adoranda
Laudamus praecordia.

This the festal day of beauty,
Bring we to God's Heart our duty:
Offerings and homage suited.

Cor amandum Salvatoris,
Mellis fortem et amoris,
Corda cuncta diligant.

Heart of mercy and of love,
Fount of sweetness from above,
Let all hearts to Thee be moved.

Cor beatum summi Regis,
Cor et vitam novæ legis,
Omnes Lingæ concinant.

Blessed Heart of Sovereign King,
Who New Law and life dost bring:
Let all tongues unite to sing.

Sit laus plena, sit immensa,
Sit perennis, sit accensa,
Ardoribus pectoris!

Let our praise be full and boundless,
Be immortal, skyless, groundless,
Kindled by the flames of love!

Laudet, canat orbis totus,
Colet, amet tota virtus
Et cordis et corporis!

Let the world with praises ring,
Let the powers of mankind sing,
Soul and body now combine!

Ora, manus, sensus, vigor,
Fides viva, purus amor,
Cor divinum consonent!

Strength and senses, voice and
    hand,
Living faith, pure love, command
All to laud this heart divine!

Flammis sacris inflammata
Corda voces atque facta,
Cor amoris prædicent!

Kindled by His sacred fire
Hearts and lips and deeds conspire
Love and praise abroad to spread!

Cor mirandum Redemptoris,
Coadunans terram cælis,
Unitatis speculum.

Heart of our Redeemer wondrous,
Linking earth to heaven splendrous,
Mirror fair of unity!

Digna sedes Trinitatis,
Plenitudo Deitatis,
Amoris miraculum.

Worthy throne of Holy Trinity,
Plenitude of the Divinity,
Miracle of love supreme.

Amoris Evangelium,
Puri cordis incendium,
Magna Dei gloria.

Love's evangel, conflagration
Of the pure heart's pure elation;
Deity's great glory.

Cæli nectar vivificans,
Cordis manna deificans;
Amor et lætitia.

Nectar from the skies, vivific,
Manna of the heart deific;
Charity and joyousness.

Cleri sacri præsidium,
Rector benigne cordium,
Nostra rege pectora!

Shield unto the sacred priesthood,
Ruling hearts from best to least
    good,
Us Thy children rule.

Fons æternæ pietatis,
Ardens fornax caritatis,
Corda flammis devora!

Fount eternal, Source of piety,
Flaming furnace, love's satiety,
With Thy fires our hearts consume!

Domus amoris aurea,
Turris amantum flammea,
Cætus nostri lex ignea,
Fons perennis gratiæ.

Golden house of glowing love,
Tower flaming from above,
Law our hearts burn to embrace,
Fountain of eternal grace.

Cor, thesaurus sanctitatis,
Abyssus humilitatis,
Thronus Dei voluntatis,
Et centrum clementiæ.

Heart, of sanctity the treasure,
And humility's vast measure,
Throne where dwells God's holy
    pleasure,
And center of mercy sweet.

Paradisus Beatorum,
Consolator afflictorum,
Pax et salus peccatorum,
Cor omnibus omnia.

Paradise of all the Blest,
Comforter, affliction's rest,
Peace that saves the sinner's fall,
Loving heart all things to all.

O Jesu, raptor cordium,
Amore flagrans mentium,
Cor tuum trahat omnium
Mentes et præcordia!

O Jesus, ravisher of hearts,
Pierce us with Thy flaming darts,
Draw our being all to Thee,
Minds and feelings utterly.

O Cor, summa benignitas,
Immensa liberalitas,
Incomprehensa caritas,
Cordis vera felicitas,
Cor esto supplicibus!

O Heart with tenderness supreme,
Boundless, generous, like a stream,
Charity unplumbed we deem.
Hearts in darkness the true beam,
Have to suppliants all a heart.

Fac nos, Jesu flammescentem
Cordis tui caritatem,
Et divinam pietatem,
Summam quoque sanctitatem
Sanctis sequi moribus!

Make us, Jesus, follow steadfast
Thy Heart's burning love in ear-
    nest,
Its most godlike piety
And its holy sanctity.
Let our lives but image Thee.

O beata Trinitas,
Cordis Jesu caritas,
Immensæ clementiæ
Immensæ sint gratiæ,
Æterna sit gloria.
Amen dicant omnia!
Amen, Alleluia.

O Most Blessed Trinity,
Heart of Jesus' Charity,
To Thy boundless mercy be
Thanks returned in boundless fee.
Let us all say: Amen, So be it!
God be praised. Fiat.

Sequentia sancti Evangelii secundum Joannem (c. 15)

In illo tempore: dixit Jesus discipulis suis: Sicut dilexit me Pater, et ego dilexi vos. Manete in dilectione mea. Si præcepta mea servaveritis, manebitis in dilectione mea, sicut et ego Patris mei præcepta servavi et maneo in ejus dilectione. Hæc locutus sum vobis, ut gaudium meum in vobis sit, et gaudium vestrum impleatur. Hoc est præceptum meum, ut diligatis invicem, sicut dilexi vos. Majorem hac dilectionem nemo habet ut animam suam ponat quis pro amicis suis. Vos amici mei estis, si feceritis quæ ego præcipio vobis. Jam non dicam vos servos: quia servus nescit quid faciat Dominus ejus. Vos autem dixi amicos, quia omnia quæcumque audivi a Patre meo nota feci vobis. Non vos me elegistis, sed ego elegi vos, et posui vos, ut eatis, et fructum afferatis, et fructus vester maneat; ut quodcumque petieritis Patrem in nomine meo, det vobis. Hæc mando vobis ut diligatis invicem.

Continuation of the holy Gospel according to St. John (c. 15)

At that time, Jesus said to his disciples: As the Father hath loved me, I also have loved you. Abide in my love. If you keep my commandments, you shall abide in my love: as I also have kept my Father's commandments and do abide in His love. These things I have spoken to you, that my joy may be in you and your joy may be filled. This is my commandment, that you love one another, as I have loved you. Greater love than this no man hath, that a man lay down his life for his friends. You are my friends if you do the things that I command you. I will not now call you servants for the servant knoweth not what his lord doth. But I have called you friends: because all things, whatsoever I have heard of my Father, I have made known to you. You have not chosen me: but I have chosen you; and have appointed you that you should go and should bring forth fruit; and your fruit should remain; that whatsoever you shall ask of the Father in my name, He may give it you. These things I command you that you love one another.

Credo
Offertorium (ps. 19)

Memor sit Dominus omnis sacrificii tui, amantissime Jesu; et holocaustum tuum pingue fiat; tribuat tibi secundum Cor tuum, et omne consilium tuum confirmet.

Creed
Offertory (Ps. 19)

May the Lord be mindful of all thy sacrifices: and may thy burnt offering be made fat. May He give thee according to thy own heart; and confirm all thy counsels.

Secreta

Cordibus nostris, omnipotens Deus, Spiritum et Cor dilectissimi Filii tui Jesu benignus infunde: ut nos, uno spiritu et uno corde cum ipso, unam eamdemque hostiam offerentes, tibi etiam nosmetipsos, atque omnia nostra immolare mereamur. Per eumdem Dominum.

Præfatio Nativitatis

Communio. Per Cor tuum, amantissime Jesu, amoris et doloris impetu pro nobis in morte disruptum, exaudi clamantes ad te, et miserere nobis, et posside cor nostrum in æternum.

Postcommunio. Exaudi, quæsumus, clementissime Pater, preces familiæ tuæ toto corde tibi prostratæ, et præsta: ut amantissimi Cordis dilectissimi Filii tui ardentissima caritas cordis nostri penetralia infundens, divinum nobis fervorem præbeat, nosque sui participes potenter efficiat: ut, eodem Corde sacratissimo interveniente, corda nostra in igne tui amoris, atque in flamma æternæ caritatis, tibi jugiter immolentur, et justa eorum desideria compleantur. Per eumdem Dominum.

Secret

Almighty God, bestow upon our hearts the spirit of the Heart of Jesus, Thy beloved Son, so that we who offer in the same spirit and heart with Him, one and the same sacrifice, may merit to be immolated in Thy honor with all that belongs to us. Through Our Lord.

Preface of the Nativity

Communion. O most loving Jesus, by Thy Heart, which was broken for us at the hour of Thy death, by the violence of Thy suffering and love, hear our cries to Thee, have mercy on us and possess our hearts forever.

Postcommunion. Hear, we beseech Thee, O most merciful Father, the prayers of Thy servant prostrate before Thee, and grant that the burning charity of the most loving Heart of Jesus, Thy beloved Son, penetrating to the very depths of our heart, may enkindle in us a heavenly ardor and make us share abundantly in His virtue that by the intercession of this same holy Heart our hearts may be continually immolated in the fire of Thy love and in the flame of eternal charity, and their just desires accomplished. Through the same Lord.

OFFICE OF THE SACRED HEART OF JESUS

FIRST VESPERS

Psalm. de Dom., sed loco ultimi,
Psalm. Laudate Dominum Omnes
gentes

Ant. 1. Jesus, ingrediens mundum, dicit: In capite libri scriptum est de me, ut faciam voluntatem tuam: Deus meus volui, et legem tuam in medio Cordis mei, alleluia.

Ant. 2. Venite ad me, filioli: in caritate enim perpetua dilexi vos: ideo attraxi vos ad Cor meum, fontem omnium bonorum, alleluia.

Ant. 3. Ego diligentes me diligo, et deliciæ meæ esse cum filiis hominum, alleluia.

Ant. 4. Cor meum caritas est; qui manet in caritate, in Corde meo manet, et Cor meum manet in eo, alleluia.

Ant. 5. Qui vicerit, dabo ei sedere mecum in throno meo: et scribam super eum nomen meum, et cor unum mecum habebit in aeternum, alleluia.

Psalms for Sunday. Last psalm.
Laudate Dominum

Ant. 1. Jesus coming into the world said: In the head of the Book it is written of Me that I should do Thy will; I have willed it, O my God, and Thy law is in the midst of My Heart, alleluia.

Ant. 2. Come to me, my little children, for I have loved you with an eternal love; therefore, have I drawn you to my Heart, which is the source of all good, alleluia.

Ant. 3. I love those who love me and my delight is to be with the children of men, alleluia.

Ant. 4. My Heart is charity itself; he who dwelleth in charity dwells in My Heart and My Heart dwelleth in him, alleluia.

Ant. 5. He who is victorious shall sit on my throne; I shall write my name upon him and he shall have but one heart with Me for all eternity, alleluia.

Capitulum (3 Regum 9)

Sanctificavi mihi donum hanc, ut ponerem nomen meum ibi in sempiternum, et erunt oculi mei et Cor meum ibi cunctis diebus.

Chapter (3 Kings 9)

I have sanctified this house, to put my name there for ever; and my eyes and my Heart shall be there always.

Hymnus

Jesu, Paterni Pectoris
Et Virginis Cor unicum,
Cordis tui mirabilis
Omnes canant præconium.

Hymn

O Heart of Jesus, solely one,
Of Father and of Virgin born,
Receive the praises now begun:
Let men with song Thy Heart adorn!

O Cor, amator Numinis,
Amore Patris igneum,
Amore flagrans Virginis,
Amore nostri saucium.

Heart, lover of the Godhead here,
The Father draws Thy flame above,
Heart burning for the Virgin fair,
And pierced for us with ardent love.

Nam sponsa, Corde saucia,
Te vulneratum vulnerat:
Te dissecat mors impia,
Et hasta dire perforat.

Thy Spouse, whose heart is torn with pain,
Doth wound Thee in the wounds Thou hast.
Then wicked death rends Thee in twain,
The piercing lance strikes deep at last.

Ave, dolorum victima,
Centrum Crucis, Rex Martyrum:
Fac nostra sit Crux gloria,
Amor, corona, gaudium.

Hail! Victim of all woes enthroned
Upon the Cross, the Martyrs' King!
Make Thou the Cross a joy entoned,
The crown and glory that we sing.

O Cor, amore saucium,
Amore corda saucia:
Vitale nectar cælitum,
Amore nos inebria.

O Heart, transfixed with wounds of love,
Pierce every heart with love for Thee.
Refresh our thirst from high above
With nectar sweet and heavenly.

Tu caritatis hostia,
Mortalium salvatio,
Aperta cunctis gratia,
Et omnium redemptio.

The host of love divine art Thou,
Salvation for all mortals here,
The way of grace lies open now,
For all redemption is brought near.

Venite, gentes, currite
Ad Cor Patris mitissimum:
Omnes amat, confidite,
Amoris est incendium.

Draw nigh, all peoples, hasten near,
And in God's gentle heart confide.
He loves each one with love so dear,
It burns like flames spread far and
    wide.

En cernitur patescere
Fornax amoris flammea:
Flammis volo me tradere,
Me devoret mors ignea.

Behold how to our yearning orbs
Love's furnace opens glowing wide!
We long to burn till it absorbs
Our being in its flaming tide.

Amor, Pater clementiæ,
Amor Redemptor omnium,
Amor, Deus, fons gratiæ,
Regnes in omme sæculum.
                Amen.

O Love, of mercy sweet the Sire,
O Love, Redeemer of all men,
O Love, of God the grace and fire,
Forever and forever reign! Amen.

V. Sic nos dilexit Jesus, ut daret nobis Cor suum.

   R. Gratias ei super inenarrabili dono ejus.

V. Jesus so loved us as to give us His Heart.

   R. Let us give thanks for this ineffable gift.

Ad Magnificat

   Ant. Gaude, Maria, Mater Redemptoris: ecce vulnerasti et rapuisti Cor ejus, et factum est Cor tuum: ipsumque nobis dedisti, ut cum Patre et Matre cor unum habeamus, alleluia.

At the Magnificat

   Ant. Rejoice O Mary, Mother of the Redeemer. Behold Thou hast wounded and ravished His Heart, which has become thine, and thou hast given it to us, that we may have but one heart with our Father and our Mother. Alleluia.

Oremus

   Pater misericordiarum, et Deus totius consolationis, qui, propter nimiam caritatem qua dilexisti nos, dilectissimi Filii tui Cor amantissimum nobis ineffabili bonitate donasti, ut te uno corde cum ipso perfecte diligamus: præsta, quæsumus; ut cordibus nostris inter se et cum Corde Jesu in unum consummatis, omnia nostra in humilitate et caritate ejus fiant, atque, ipso interve-

Let us pray

   Father of mercy and God of all consolation, who by the exceeding love with which Thou hast loved us, hast given with ineffable goodness, the Heart of Thy beloved Son, so that having but one heart with Him we may love Thee perfectly, grant, we beseech Thee, that our hearts, being consumed in unity among themselves and with the Heart of Jesus, we may perform

niente, justa cordis nostri desideria compleantur. Per eumdem Dominum.

all our works in His humility and charity, and that by His mediation, the just desires of our hearts may be accomplished. Through the same Lord.

MATINS

Invit. Jesu Cor amantissimum, venite, adoremus: Qui est amor et vita nostra.

Invit. Come, let us adore the most loving Heart of Jesus, our love and our life.

Psalmus. Venite, exsultemus Domino.

Psalm. 94. Come, let us praise the Lord.

Hymnus
Verbum caro, rex cordium,
Cordis tui miracula
Linguis canantur omnium
Miraculorum maxima.

Hymn
O Word made flesh, of hearts the King,
Let all, who see the wonders great
Of Thy vast Heart, with one voice sing;
The grandeur of Thy Heart relate.

Ave, Patris mirabilis
Et Unici Cor unicum;
Origo sacri Flaminis,
Terræ polique vinculum.

All hail, O Heart of wondrous line,
Of Son and Father twain but one,
O source of Holy Spirit, Thine
To bind together earth and sun.

Quam magna fers mysteria,
Immensa gaza cælitum:
Amoris arca regia,
Ecclesiæ sacrarium!

What mysteries great Thou dost enfold,
O boundless treasure from above,
O royal ark of love foretold,
The Church's holy place of love.

Pars nostra, spes et gaudium,
Cætusque nostri gloria:
Cor, flamma, dux, oraculum,
Origo, finis, omnia.

Thou art our portion, hope and weal,
Thy glory of our multitude;
Our source and end, our heart and zeal,
Our leader and our plenitude.

Quam mira Jesu gratia!
Nos Corde toto diligit;
Solvamus ut nos debita,
Nobis suum Cor tradidit.

O qualis haec dignatio!
Dat Cor Mariæ Filius,
Dat Cor Mariæ Filio,
Utrumque dant volentibus.

O te volo, Cor flammeum,
Tu semper intus ardeas:
Fons omnium charismatum,
Totum per orbem diffluas.

O Cor meum, Cor unicum,
Virtus, salus, fiducia,
Thesaure, sol, et jubilum,
In te mihi sunt omnia.

Amor, Pater clementiæ,
Amor, Redemptor omnium,
Amor, Deus, fons gratiæ,
Regnes in omne sæculum.

We marvel at His wondrous grace!
His Heart He gives with total love,
From bondage frees the human race
And pays our debts to heaven above.

Oh, what a noble act is done!
The Son to Mary gives His Heart
And Mary hers unto the Son;
To all who will they both impart.

O Heart of flame, I long for Thee
To burn forevermore within;
That Thou the source of graces free
Should overwhelm the whole world's sin.

O Thou my Heart, sole Heart, unique,
Salvation, strength, and treasure, all;
My sun and joy and trust to seek
In Thee, and finding Thee find all!

O Love, of mercy sweet the Sire,
O Love, Redeemer of all men,
O Love, of God the grace and fire,
Forever and forever reign. Amen.

In Primo Nocturno

Ant. Christus Jesus, a sinu Patris amore nimio egressus, exsultavit ut gigas ad currendam viam: nec est qui se abscondat a calore dilectionis Dei.

First Nocturn

Ant. Jesus Christ with exceeding love, came forth from the bosom of His Father, He rejoiced as a giant to run His course, nor is there anyone who is hid from the heat of His love.

Psalmus 18. Cæli enarrant.

Ant. Memor sit Pater omnis sacrificii tui, O Rex amoris, et tribuat tibi secundum Cor tuum.

Ant. May the Father be mindful of all Thy Sacrifices and reward Thee according to the desires of Thy Heart.

Psalmus 19. *Exaudiat te.*

Ant. Desiderio desideravi meipsum et in victimam et in escam dare vobis: et desiderium Cordis mei tribuit mihi Pater.

Ant. With desire I have desired to give myself to you as Victim and as Food; and the Father has granted me the desire of My Heart.

Psalmus 20. *Domine, in virtute.*

V. Sic nos dilexit Jesus, ut daret nobis Cor suum.
R. Gratias ei super inenarrabili dono ejus.

V. Jesus so loved man as to give us His Heart.
R. Thanks to Him for this ineffable gift.

Lectio I: De Ezechiele Propheta (c. 36)

Sanctificabo nomen meum magnum ut sciant gentes quia ego Dominus, ait Dominus exercituum, cum sanctificatus fuero in vobis coram eis. Tollam quippe vos de gentibus, et congregabo vos de universis terris, et adducam vos in terram vestram. Et effundam super vos aquam mundam, et mundabimini ab omnibus inquinamentis vestris, et ab universis idolis vestris mundabo vos. Et dabo vobis cor novum, et spiritum novum ponam in medio vestri: et auferam cor lapideum de carne vestra, et dabo vobis cor carneum, et spiritum meum ponam in medio vestri.

Lesson I: Ezechiel (c. 36)

I will sanctify my great name that the Gentiles may know that I am the Lord, saith the Lord of hosts, when I shall be sanctified in you before their eyes. For I will take you from among the Gentiles and will gather you together out of all the countries and will bring you into your own land. And I will pour upon you clean water and you shall be cleansed from all your filthiness: and I will cleanse you from all your idols. And I will give you a new heart and put a new spirit within you: and I will take away the stony heart out of your flesh and will give you a heart of flesh. And I will put my spirit in the midst of you.

R. Elegi et vocavi Filium meum Jesum, virum voluntatis meæ, et secundum Cor meum. Quæ placita sunt mihi facit semper corde magno et animo volenti.

R. I have chosen and have called my Son, Jesus, a man of my will and according to my own Heart, for He always does what is pleasing to Me with generous Heart and resolute will.

V. Paratum Cor meum, Pater sancte, paratum Cor meum, ut faciam omnes voluntates tuas.—Quæ.

V. My Heart is ready, Holy Father, my Heart is ready to do all that Thou willest.

Lectio II: De Canticis Canticorum (c. 3)

Ferculum fecit sibi rex Salomon de lignis Libani: columnas ejus fecit argentas, reclinatorium aureum, ascensum purpureum: media caritate constravit, propter filias Jerusalem. Egredimini et videte, filiæ Sion, regem Salomonem in diademate quo coronavit illum mater sua in die desponsationis illius et in die lætitiæ Cordis ejus.

R. Dabo vobis spiritum et cor novum; Spiritum et Cor meum ponam in medio vestri: Ut diligatis Deum corde magno et animo volenti.
V. Quoniam estis filii Dei et membra Christi, posuit Deus Spiritum suum et Cor Filii sui in medio vestri; ut cum Patre et Capite vestro sit vobis spiritus unus et cor unum.—Ut.

Lectio III: Ibid. (c. 4)

Veni de Libano, sponsa mea, veni de Libano, veni. Coronaberis de capite Amana, de vertice Sanir et Hermon, de cubilibus leonum, de montibus pardorum. Vulnerasti Cor meum, soror mea sponsa, vulnerasti Cor meum, in uno oculorum tuorum, et in uno crine colli tui. Veni in hortum meum, soror mea sponsa: messui myrrham meam cum aromatibus meis: comedi favum cum melle meo, bibi vinum meum cum

Lesson II: Canticle of Canticles (c. 3)

King Solomon hath made him a litter of the wood of Libanus. The pillars thereof he made of silver, the seat of gold, the going up of purple: the midst he covered with charity for the daughters of Jerusalem. Go forth, ye daughters of Sion, and see King Solomon in the diadem wherewith his mother crowned him in the day of his espousals, and in the day of the joy of his heart.

R. I will give you a new spirit and a new heart and will put my spirit and my heart in the midst of you that you may love God with a generous heart and resolute will.
V. For you are children of God and members of Christ. God has put His spirit and the Heart of His Son in the midst of you that you may be one in heart and spirit with your Father and head that you may love God with a generous Heart and resolute will.

Lesson III: Ibid. (c. 4)

Come from Libanus, my spouse, come from Libanus, come; thou shalt be crowned from the top of Amana, from the top of Sanir and Hermon, from the dens of the lions, from the mountains of leopards. Thou hast wounded my Heart, my Sister, my Spouse; Thou hast wounded my Heart, with one of thy eyes, and with one hair of thy neck. Come into my garden, my Sister, my Spouse, I have gathered

lacte meo: comedite, amici, et bibite, et inebriamini, carissimi.

my myrrh with aromatical spices. I have eaten the honeycomb with my honey. I have drunk my wine with my milk. Eat, my friends, drink and be inebriated, my dearly beloved.

R. Pater misericordiarum, et Deus totius consolationis, benedicant tibi omnes virtutes tuæ. Quia sic nos dilexisti, ut Filium tuum unigenitum, et omnia cum ipso nobis donares.

V. Ut cum ipso Cor unum habentes, te uno corde diligamus, secundum magnitudinem bonitatis tuæ.—Quia. Gloria Patri. Quia.

R. Father of Mercies and God of all consolation, may all Thy powers bless Thee, for Thou hast so loved us to give us Thy only Begotten Son and all things together with Him.

V. That having but one heart with Him, we might love Thee with one heart, according to Thy infinite goodness. For Thou hast so loved us as to give us Thy only Begotten Son and all things together with Him. For Thou hast.—Glory be the Father.

In Secundo Nocturno

Ant. Unam petii a Domino hanc requiram: ut in die malorum abscondat et protegat me in abscondito Cordis sui.

Second Nocturn

Ant. One thing only have I asked of the Lord: this will I seek that He may shelter me from evil and hide me in the very depths of His Heart.

Psalmus 26. *Dominus illuminatio mea.*

Ant. In capite Libri scriptum est de me, ut faciam voluntatem tuam: Deus meus, volui, et legem tuam in medio Cordis mei.

Ant. In the Head of the Book it is written of Me that I should do Thy will; I have willed it and Thy law is in the midst of My Heart.

Psalmus 39, *Expectans expectavi Dominum.*

Ant. Paratum Cor meum, Pater sancte, paratum Cor meum: confitebor tibi in cithara Cordis mei in sempiternum.

Ant. My heart is ready, Holy Father, my heart is ready. I shall sing Thy praises forever.

Psalmus 56, *Miserere mei, Deus, miserere mei.*

V. Sicut dilexit me Pater et ego dilexi vos.

R. Et vos manete in dilectione mea.

Lectio IV: Sermo Sancti Bonaventuræ Episcopi. Ex tractatu de Passione Dom. super istud Joan. "Ego sum vitis vera." (c. 3)

Foderunt Judaei et perfoderunt, non solum manus, sed et pedes, latus quoque; et sanctissimi Cordis intima furoris lancea perforaverunt, quod jamdudum amoris lancea fuerat vulneratum. Vulnerasti, inquit in Canticis amoris sponsus, Cor meum, soror mea, sponsa, vulnerasti Cor meum. Vulnerat Cor tuum, Domine Jesu, sponsa tua, amica tua, soror tua. Quid necessarium fuit illud ab inimicis tuis ultra vulnerari? Quid agitis, o inimici? Si vulneratum est Cor dulcis Jesu, quid secundum vulnus apponitis? An ignoratis quod uno vulnere tactum Cor emoritur, et fit insensibile? Mortuum est Cor Domini Jesu, quia vulneratum: possedit vulnus amoris; possedit mors amoris Domini Cor, sponsi Jesu: quomodo mors altera introibit?

R. Omnia mihi tradita sunt a Patre meo. Et sic Pater dilexit mundum, ut Filium suum unigenitum

V. As the Father has loved me and I have loved you.

R. And you shall dwell in my love.

Lesson IV: Sermon of Saint Bonaventure Bishop. From the Treatise on the Passion of Our Lord. Commentary on Saint John's words: "I am the true vine." (c. 3)

The Jews dug and pierced not only His hands and feet, but also His side; they pierced to the very core with the lance of rage His most Holy Heart which had long since been wounded by the lance of love. Thou hast wounded my heart, says the spouse of love in the Canticles; my Sister, my Spouse, thou hast wounded my heart, O Lord Jesus, Thy Spouse, Thy beloved, Thy sister, wounds Thy heart; why was it necessary that it should be wounded by thine enemies? What are you doing, O ye enemies? Since the sweet Heart of Jesus has been wounded, why do you add a second wound? Do you not know that the heart dies from one wound and becomes insensible? The Heart of the Lord Jesus is dead, for it has been wounded. It has been wounded by love. The Heart of the Lord Jesus has died of love for His Spouse. Why should another death enter in?

R. All things have been given to Me by My Father and as the Father so loved the world as to

daret; itaque omnia vestra mea sunt. * Præbete ergo mihi cor vestrum, filioli, et dabo vobis Cor meum.

V. Cor nostrum in manu tua, O Domine Jesu, secundum magnitudinem brachii tui posside illud in æternum.—Præbete.

Lectio V

Vide quanta sit vis amoris domum Cordis obtinentis, et per vulnus dulcissimum occidentis non solum in Domino Jesu, sed et in servis ipsius. Veniamus ad Martyres: feriuntur, et gaudent; occiduntur, et triumphant. Quare? Quia morte caritatis, intus in corde, jamdudum mortui peccatis, mortui mundo, tanquam insensibiles facti, nec minas nec tormenta sentire potuerunt. Sed quia semel venimus ad Cor dulcissimum Jesu, et bonum est nos hic esse, ne sinamus nos facile avelli ab eo, de quo scriptum est: Recedentes a te in terra scribentur. Accedamus ergo ad eum, et exsultabimus, et lætabimur in illo, memores Cordis ipsius.

R. Cor Jesu, verum altare holocausti, in quo ignis divinus semper accenditur. * Afferte, filii Dei, afferte corda vestra, ut in hoc altare Deo jugiter immolentur.

V. Dirumpe, Domine, vincula mea, et tibi sacrificabo hostium laudis et amoris.—Afferte.

give His only Begotten Son, so all you have is mine and all I have is yours. Therefore, My children, give me your hearts and I will give you Mine.

V. Our Heart is in Thy hands, O Lord Jesus, according to the might of Thy arm; possess it forever.

Lesson V

Behold how great is the violence of His Heart's love, obtaining a dwelling and bringing death by means of this sweetest wound not only to the Lord Jesus, but also to His servants. Look at the Martyrs; they are tortured and they rejoice; they are slain and they triumph. Why? Because their hearts by the death of charity have long since been dead to sin, dead to the world; they had become insensible so that they could feel neither threats nor torments. But since we have once come to the Sweetest Heart of Jesus, and it is good for us to be there, let us not suffer ourselves to be easily drawn away from it, of whom it is written: "Withdrawing from Thee they will be written on the ground." Let us hasten to Him, therefore, and exult and rejoice in Him being mindful of His Heart.

R. The Heart of Jesus is a true sacrificial altar on which the Divine fire is ever burning. Children of God, bring your hearts that they may be constantly immolated to God on this altar.

V. O Lord, loose my bonds and I shall offer Thee a sacrifice of praise and love.

Lectio VI

O quam bonum et quam jucundum habitare in Corde Jesu! Bonus hesaurus, bona margarita Cor tuum, bone Jesu, quam fosso agro tui corporis invenimus. Quis hanc margaritam abjiciat? Quin potius dabo omnia, omnes cogitationes et affectus mentis commutabo, et comparabo illam mihi, jactans omnem cogitatum meum in Cor Domini Jesu, et sine fallacia illud me enutriet. Ad hoc templum, ad hæc sancta sanctorum, ad hanc arcam testimenti adorabo, et laudabo nomen Domini, dicens cum David: Inveni cor meum, inquit, ut orem Deum meum. Et ego inveni Cor regis, fratris et amici, benigni Jesu. Et numquid non adorabo? Orabo utique; Cor enim illius meum est. Audacter dicam, si enim caput meum Christus est quomodo quod capitis mei est, non meum est? Sicut ergo oculi capitis mei corporalis, mei oculi vere sunt; ita et spiritualis Cor, Cor meum est. Bene ergo mihi: ego vere cum Jesu cor unum habeo. Et quid mirum, cum multitudinis credentium fuerit cor unum?

R. Fornax amoris Cor tuum, o amantissime Jesu.* Afferte corda vestra in hanc fornacem, ut in igne divini amoris et in flamma æternæ caritatis consumantur.

V. Beati qui in ignem æternum

Lesson VI

Oh, how good and delightful it is to dwell in the Heart of Jesus! Thy Heart, O good Jesus, is a precious treasure, a precious pearl which we have found by digging the field of Thy Body. Who will cast aside this pearl? Nay, rather, I will give all I have, I will exchange all my thoughts and desires and purchase it. I will cast all my care on the Heart of the Lord Jesus and He will provide for me without fail. I will adore in this temple, this Holy of Holies, this Ark of the Testament, and I will praise the Name of the Lord, saying, with David, "I have found my heart that I may pray to my God. And I have found the heart of my King, my Brother, my Friend, the benign Jesus, and why shall I not adore?" Assuredly I shall pray. For His Heart is mine. I will say it boldly, for if Christ is my Head, is not what belongs to my Head mine? Therefore, as the eyes of my corporal head are truly my eyes, so is my spiritual heart my heart. Therefore, it is well with me: truly I have but one Heart with Jesus and what wonder that there should be but one heart with the multitude of believers.

R. Thy Heart, O most loving Jesus, is a furnace of love. Bring your hearts to this furnace that they may be consumed in the fire of Divine Love and in the flames of eternal charity.

V. Blessed are they who are

hujus fornacis mittuntur.—Afferte.
Gloria Patri.—Afferte.

In Tertio Nocturno

Ant. Accedamus ad Cor altissimum Jesu, ut per ipsum, et cum ipso, et in ipso, exaltemus et diligamus Deum, secundum multitudinem magnitudinis ejus.

Psalmus 63. *Exaudi, Deus.*

Ant. Qui adhæret Domino Jesu, unum cor et unus spiritus est: et de immenso thesauro Cordis ejus accipiet immensa bona.

Psalmus 72. *Quam bonus Israel Deus.*

Ant. Turbatum et anxiatum est Cor meum: deficit in dolore vita mea, et anni mei in gemitibus, propter nimiam caritatem qua dilexi vos.

Psalmus 142. *Domine exaudi orationem meam.*

V. Vivat Cor Jesu, Rex cordium.

R. Et regnet super omnia corda in æternum.

Lectio VII: Lectio sancti Evangelii secundum Joannem (Cap. 15)

In illo tempore: Dixit Jesus discipulis suis: Sicut dilexit me Pater, et ego dilexi vos; manete in dilectione mea. Et reliqua.

Homilia sancti Joannis Chrysostomi (In Joann. Homil. 76.)

Sicut dilexit me Pater, et ego dilexi vos. Hic jam magis secundum hominem loquitur. Nam qui mori

placed in the eternal fire of this furnace. Glory be the Father.

Third Nocturn

Ant. Let us hasten to the most holy Heart of Jesus, that through Him, and with Him, and in Him, we may praise God according to the greatness of His Majesty.

Ant. He who follows Jesus, our Lord, is one with Him in heart and spirit and will receive great gifts from the vast treasury of His Heart.

Ant. My Heart is troubled and anxious, my life is spent in sorrow and my years in groaning on account of the exceeding love wherewith I have loved you.

V. Live, Heart of Jesus, King of Hearts.

R. And reign over all hearts forever.

Lesson VII: The Gospel of St. John (C. 15)

At that time Jesus said to His disciples: "As the Father has loved me and I have loved you; Abide in my love.

Homily of St. John Chrysostom

As the Father has loved Me and I have loved you. Now here He speaks more after the manner of

voluit; qui servos, inimicos, hostes, in tanto honore habere dignatus est, et in cœlum adduxit, quomodo dilectionis mensuram ostendit? Si ergo vos diligo, confidite; sed ne inde negligentes faceret, vide quomodo eos rursus excitat: Manete, inquit, in dilectione mea. Hoc in vestra est potestate. Quomodo autem hoc erit? Si præcepta mea servaveritis, sicut ego præcepta Patris mei servavi. Considera autem quanta eos auctoritate alloquatur; non enim dixit: Manete in dilectione Patris, sed mea. Inde vero ne dicerent: Quando nos omnibus inimicos reddidisti, tunc nos dimittis, tunc discedis; hoc negat; sed ita se eis, modo velint, conglutinari dicit, ut palmes viti.

man; for, in willing to die, in deigning to hold slaves and enemies in such honor and in bringing them to Heaven, He showed the measure of His love. If, therefore, I love you, have confidence; but lest He make them negligent, see how He again encourages them; abide, He says, in my love. This is in your power. But how shall this be? If you keep My commandments as I have kept the commandments of My Father. Consider with what authority He speaks to them, for He does not say: dwell in the love of My Father, but dwell in my love. Then lest they say with truth: first, Thou makest the world our enemy and then Thou dost cast us off and abandon us. This He denies; but He says that He is as closely united to them, provided they wish it, as the branches to the vine.

R. Thronus meus flamma ignis: fluvius igneus rapidusque egreditur a facie mea. Et ego ignis consumens, ignem veni mittere terram. * Et quid volo nisi ut accendatur.

V. O ignis qui semper ardes, et nunquam extingueris. O amor qui semper ferves, et nunquam extingueris! O amor qui semper ferves, et nunquam tepescis, accende me totum, ut totus diligam te!—Et.

R. My throne is flaming fire; a fiery and swift flowing stream comes forth from My Face, and I consuming fire have come to cast fire upon the earth; and what will I, but that it be enkindled.

V. O fire which ever burnest and is never extinguished, O Love which is ever fervent and never grows tepid, inflame me wholly that I may love Thee wholly.

Lectio VIII

In me, inquit, respicite. Diligit me Pater, et tamen mors acerbissima mihi subeunda proponitur. Non igitur vos nunc relinquo, eo quod non diligam. Nam si ego mo-

Lesson VIII

Look upon me, He says. The Father loves Me, and yet it is decreed that I must suffer a most cruel death. Therefore, I am not leaving you because I do not love

rior, nec tamen propterea a Patre non amari conjicio; sic neque vos, ob discessum meum, perturbari oportet. Si in dilectione mea manseritis, nihil vobis nocere poterit. Magnum namque et inseparabile quiddam est dilectio, quæ non tantum verbis, sed re exhibenda est. Itaque cum ipse nos Deo reconciliaverit, in amore perstemus. Cum diligere ipse inceperit, nos saltem prosequamur. Cum ipse non sui commodi gratia, nullius enim eget, nos saltem ad nostram utilitatem diligamus. Cum ipse inimicos, nos saltem eum, qui amicus est, amore prosequamur.

R. O admirabilis Cordis Jesu caritas, qui pro crucificentibus se oravit, dicens; * Pater, dimitte illis, non enim sciunt quid faciunt.

V. Filioli, ponite corda vestra in caritate Cordis mei, ut diligatis inimicos vestros, et oretis pro persequentibus vos.—Pater. — G l o r i a Patri.

Lectio IX

Hæc locutus sum vobis, ut gaudium meum in vobis sit, et gaudium vestrum impleatur; hoc est, ne discedatis a me, neve a cursu desistatis. Vos amici mei estis, si feceritis quæ præcipio vobis. Jam non dico vos servos, quia servus nescit quid faciat Dominus ejus; vos autem dixi amicos, quia omnia quæ audivi a Patre meo, nota feci vobis. Nihil aliud his verbis innuit, quam maximi amoris indi-

you. For if I die I do not, therefore, consider that I am not loved by the Father; so neither should you be disturbed on account of my departure. If you abide in My love no harm can come to you. For love is mighty and close-clinging and has to be shown not only by the lips but from the very depths of the heart. So since He has reconciled us to God, let us at least continue. Since He loved us not *for His own advantage, for He has* need of no one, let us by all means love to our advantage. Since He loved His enemies let us love him who is our Friend.

R. O admirable charity of the Heart of Jesus, who didst pray for Thy executioners, saying Father, forgive them, for they know not what they do.

V. Children, place your hearts in the charity of My Heart, that you may love your enemies and pray for your persecutors. Father, forgive them—Glory be to the Father.

Lesson IX

These things have I spoken to you, that My joy may be in you and that your joy may be full; depart not from me nor tire of the race. You are My friends if you do what I command you. I do not now call you servants, for the servant knoweth not what His Master doeth; but I have called you friends, for all things which I have heard from My Father I have revealed to you. These words are nothing else than

cium, quod arcana Patris cum eis communicaverit. Cum autem omnia dicit, de his intelligendum quæ eos audire conveniat. Ecce quot modis suam proponit dilectionem, cum et secreta Patris eis aperuerit, cum in amore prævenerit, cum pro ipsis tot mala patiatur, cumque perpetuo cum ipsis se permansurum ostendit.

Te Deum laudamus.

AD LAUDES

Ant. O altitudo divitiarum caritatis Jesu! quam incomprehensibilia sunt opera ejus, et amabiles viæ ejus!

Psalmi de Dominica.

Ant. O amor admirabilis, tu Filium Dei pro nobis de sinu Patris egredi, in sinu Matris infantem fieri, cum hominibus in terris conversari, et mortem pati acerbissimum fecisti! alleluia.

Ant. O dilectio ineffabilis! Ecce Cor Jesu, amoris et doloris impetu, pro nobis in morte disruptum est. Gratias ei super inenarrabili caritate ejus.

Ant. O amor amorum! carnem suam nobis in cibum, sanguinem in potum, in pretium, in lavacrum, et semetipsum in Patrem, in sponsum, in caput, in Cor, et in præmium donavit æternum. Gratias ei super immensis Cordis ejus donis.

a proof of the greatest love in that He should communicate to them the secrets of His Father. But when He says "all" we are to understand "what it was meet for them to hear." See in how many ways He proves His love since He reveals to them the secrets of the Father. He is beforehand with them in love. He endures so many sufferings for them and declares that He will remain with them forever.

Te Deum laudamus.

LAUDS

Ant. O the depths of the riches of the charity of Jesus, how incomprehensible are His works, how amiable His ways!

Psalms for Sunday.

Ant. O admirable love, Thou didst draw the Son of God from the bosom of His Father, to become man for us, in the womb of His Mother, to speak with men upon earth and to suffer a most cruel death.

Ant. O ineffable love, behold the Heart of Jesus crushed for us in death by the violence of His love and sorrow. Infinite thanks to Him for His ineffable charity.

Ant. O love of loves! He has given us His flesh to eat, His Blood to drink, to redeem us and to cleanse us; He has given Himself as Head, Heart and eternal reward. Thanks to Him for the immense gifts of His Heart.

Ant. Benedictum Cor tuum, O bone Jesu, super quod discipulus dilectus recumbens fluenta Evangelii amoris tui, nobis effundenda, potavit, alleluia.

Ant. Blessed is Thy Heart, O good Jesus, on which the Beloved disciple reposing, drank the flowing waters of the Gospel which He afterwards poured out for us, alleluia.

Capitulum: (3 Reg. 9)

Sanctificavi mihi domum hanc, ut ponerem nomen meum ibi in sempiternum, et erunt oculi mei et Cor meum ibi cunctis diebus.

Chapter: (3 Kings 9)

I have sanctified this house, to put my name there for ever: and my eyes and my Heart shall be there always.

Hymnus

Quid Corde Regis cordium
Coli potest amantius?
Cordi Patris charismatum
Quid Corde Nati carius?

Hymn

What heart more worthy can we find
To worship than our loving King?
What dearer to the Father's mind
Than His Own Heart for us to sing?

Ave, Cor, aula Numinis,
Thesaure, cælum, gloria,
Amor Parentis Virginis,
Amor triumphans omnia.

O Heart, we hail Thee, richest treasure,
Heaven's glory, Godhead's hall,
Love for Virgin, passing measure,
Love triumphant over all.

Memento, dilectissime,
Amoris ardentissimi,
Qui Patris ortum pectore
Pro me dedit te Virgini.

O Heart loved far beyond the rest,
Be mindful of that love divine,
Which flowed from out the Father's breast,
A gift to Mary, hers and mine.

Mundi recedant somnia:
Amor meus, Rex unicus,
Solus mihi sit omnia,
Jesum volo, nil amplius.

All worldly dreams now melt away;
My King shall be my love alone,
My only love, again I say
None else but Jesus is my own.

O summa Jesu caritas,
Vultu benigno respice,
Mentes draconi subditas,
Tuo redemptas sanguine.

O Jesus, height of charity,
Look down with countenance benign,
And see our minds' depravity
Redeemed by Thine own Blood divine.

Heu! quanta pro mortalibus
Tu Corde passus vulnera!
Non vana peccatoribus
Sint tanta Cordis munera.

Amanda raptor cordium,
Per Cor tuum, fac omnia,
Ad te, Creator omnium,
Sursum rapi præcordia.

O Cor, Pater viventium,
Amore fac nos vivere:
Fac in tuum, pro te, sinum
Amore vitam fundere.

Amor, Pater clementiæ,
Amor, Redemptor omnium,
Amor, Deus, fons gratiæ,
Regnes in omne sæculum.
                    Amen.

Alas! how multiplied the toll
Of wounds mankind Thy Heart
    has cost!
Thy gifts for every sinful soul
Must not by us be vainly lost.

All hearts' most loving captor Thou!
Our prayer we offer through Thy
    Heart.
To God of all creation now
Uplift our souls, uphold our part.

O Father of all those who live,
Enliven us with love of Thee.
Within Thy breast, through Thee,
    O give
Us depth of life eternally.

O Love, of mercy sweet the Sire,
O Love, Redeemer of all men.
O Love, of God the grace and fire,
Forever and forever reign!
                    Amen.

V. Omnis spiritus laudet Cor Jesu et Mariæ.
    R. Et diligant illud omnia corda.
    Ad. Bened. Ant. Benedictum sit Cor amantissimum Jesu et Mariæ, fons vivus benedictionis, fornax amoris, thronus divinæ voluntatis, sanctuarium Divinitatis, alleluia.

V. Let every soul praise the Hearts of Jesus and Mary.
    R. And every heart love them.
    Ad. Bened. Ant. Blessed be the most loving Hearts of Jesus and Mary, living fount of blessing, furnace of love, throne of the Divine Will, sanctuary of the Divinity, alleluia.

Oremus

Pater misericordiarum, et Deus totius consolationis, qui propter nimiam caritatem qua dilexisti nos, dilectissimi Filii tui Cor amantissimum nobis ineffabili bonitate donasti ut te uno corde cum ipso perfecte diligamus: præsta, quæsumus; ut cordibus nostris inter se, et cum Corde Jesu, in unum consummatis,

Let us pray

Father of Mercy and God of all consolation, who, by the exceeding love with which Thou hast loved us, hast given us with ineffable goodness the Heart of Thy beloved Son, so that having but one heart with Him we may love Thee perfectly, grant, we beseech Thee, that our hearts, being consumed in

omnia nostra in humilitate et caritate ejus fiant, atque, ipso interveniente, justa cordis nostri desideria compleantur. Per eumdem.

unity among themselves and with the Heart of Jesus, we may perform all our works in His humility and charity, and that by His mediation, the just desires of our hearts may be accomplished. Through the same.

AD PRIMAM

Ant. O altitudo divitiarum. *De Laudibus.*

R. Christi Fili.
V. Qui natus es de Maria Virgine.

PRIME

Ant. O the depths of the riches. *From Lauds.*

R. Christ, Son.
V. Who wast born of the Virgin Mary.

AD TERTIAM

Ant. O amor admirabilis.

Capit. Sanctificavi domum hanc, *ut supra.*

R. Sic nos dilexit Jesus, * ut daret nobis Cor suum. Sic nos.
V. Gratias ei super inenarrabili dono ejus. Ut daret. Gloria Patri. Sic nos.

V. Sicut dilexit me Pater, et ego dilexi vos.
R. Et vos manete in dilectione mea.

Oratio: Pater misericordiarum. *ut ad Laudes.*

TIERCE

Ant. O admirable love.

Chapter. I have sanctified . . . *as at Lauds.*

R. Jesus so loved us as to give us His Heart.
V. Thanks to Him for His ineffable gift.

V. As the Father has loved Me and I have loved you.
R. Do you abide in My love.

Oration: Father of Mercies . . . *as at Lauds.*

AD SEXTAM

Ant. O dilectio ineffabilis.

Capit: (Osee, 11) Ego quasi nutritius Ephraim, portabam eos in brachiis meis, et nescierunt quod

SEXT

Ant. O ineffable love.

Chapter: (Osee 11) I was like a foster father to Ephraim. I carried them in my arms; and they knew

curarem eos. In funiculis Adam traham eos, in vinculis caritatis.

not that I healed them. I will draw them with the cords of Adam, with the bonds of love.

R. Sicut dilexit me Pater, * et ego dilexi vos. Sicut.
V. Et vos manete in dilectione mea. Gloria Patri. Sicut.

R. As the Father hath loved Me and I have loved you.
V. Do you abide in My love. Glory be.

V. Vivat Cor Jesu, Rex cordium.

R. Et regnat super omnia corda in æternum.

V. Live the Heart of Jesus, King of Hearts.
R. And reign over all hearts forever.

AD NONAM

Ant. Benedictum Cor tuum.

Capit (Cant., 4). Vulnerasti Cor meum, soror mea, sponsa, vulnerasti Cor meum, in uno oculorum tuorum, et in uno crine colli tui.

R. Vivat Cor Jesu, * Rex cordium. Vivat Cor.
V. Et regnat super omnia corda in æternum. Rex cordium. Gloria Patri. Vivat.

V. Omnis spiritus laudet Cor Jesu et Mariæ.
R. Et diligant illud omnia corda.

NONE

Ant. Blessed is Thy Heart.

Chapter (Canticle of Canticles, 4). Thou hast wounded my Heart, my Sister, my Spouse, Thou hast wounded my Heart with one of Thy eyes, and with one hair of Thy neck.

R. Live the Heart of Jesus, King of Hearts.
V. And reign over all hearts forever.

V. Let every spirit praise the Heart of Jesus and Mary.
R. And love them forever and ever.

IN II VESPERIS

Ant. O admirabile Cor Jesu, in quo Deus Pater altissimum dilectionis et gloriæ suæ thronum constituit! alleluia.

SECOND VESPERS

Ant. O admirable Heart of Jesus in which the Father has set up the highest throne of His glory and His love.

*Ps. de Dom., sed ultimo loco,
Lauda, Jerusalem.*

Ant. O incomparabilis caritas! cum adhuc inimici essemus, dilexit nos et lavit nos a peccatis nostris in sanguine suo, alleluia.

Ant. Nolite timere, filioli, et si mulier oblita fuerit infantis sui, ego tamen non obliviscar vestri. Ecce in manibus meis et in Corde meo descripsi vos, alleluia.

Ant. Pater, quos dedisti mihi, volo ut ubi sum ego, et illi sint mecum; et nobiscum ac inter se sint cor unum, sicut et nos unum sumus, alleluia.

Ant. Filioli, implete gaudium meum, ut omnia vestra in caritate Cordis mei fiant. Paratum cor nostrum, Deus cordis nostri, paratum cor nostrum, alleluia.

Capitulum (3 Reg., 9)

Sanctificavi mihi domum hanc, ut ponerem nomen meum ibi in sempiternum, et erunt oculi mei, et Cor meum ibi cunctis diebus.

Hymnus
Flammata Jesu Pectora
Amoris igne psallimus:
Immensa læti munera
Cordis benigni pangimus.

Ave, sacerdos cordium,
Ave, Deo par victima,
Templum Deo dignissimum,
Et ara sacratissima.

O semper ara flammea,
Cunctis parata victimis,

*Psalms for Sunday. Last psalm:
Lauda Jerusalem.*

Ant. O incomparable charity, when we were still His enemies, He loved us and washed away our sins in His Blood.

Ant. Fear not, little children, though a mother forget her child, yet will I never forget you. See, I hold you engraven on My hands and in My Heart.

Ant. Father, I desire that those whom Thou hast given Me may be with Me where I am, that they may be one among themselves and one with us, as Thou and I are one.

Ant. My little children, fill My cup of joy to the full by performing all your actions in the love of My Heart. Our Heart is ready, O God of Our Heart, Our Heart is ready.

Chapter (3 Kings, 9)

I have sanctified this house, to put my name there forever: and my eyes and My Heart shall be there always.

Hymn
We sing the praise of Jesus' Heart
With fire of ardent love aflame:
With joy we tell the boundless part
His love and gifts so rightly claim.

Hail, priest of hearts and victim, hail!
Alone Thou equal art to God,
Most worthy Temple, Holy Grail,
And altar, holiest to laud.

An altar flaming, all afire,
And always set for victims there;

Tu corda tollas omnia,
Flammis litanda cœlicis.

Receive our hearts as victims, fire
And burn them in Thy heav'nly
flame.

O magna fornax Cælitum,
Æterna præbens gaudia,
Præcordiis mortalium
Cæli feras incendia.

O furnace of the heav'nly throng
Begetting us eternal joys,
In hearts of mortals kindle long
Those holy fires that purge alloys.

En illa fornax panditur:
Afferte sacris ignibus,
Afferte corda, pascitur
Fornax amanda cordibus.

Lo! how that furnace opens wide!
Bear up unto those sacred fires,
Bring up our hearts, burn'd free of
pride,
Each holy heart its flame desires.

En corda, quæ mirabilis
Fornacis ignes concrement:
Cordis faces amabilis
Terram polumque devorent.

Here offer we our hearts, and pray
This wondrous furnace shall as-
sume
And shall devour them; that the
ray
Of love both heav'n and earth consume.

Tot ergo tanti Pectoris
Omnes canant mysteria:
Cordisque tam laudabilis
Strati colant magnalia.

Thy mysteries let all men sing,
The greatness of Thy wondrous
ways.
In prostrate worship may we bring
With humble hearts unending
praise.

O Christe, fornax cordium,
Immerge flammis supplices:
Amor vorax amantium,
Fac nos amoris martyres.

O Christ, Thou furnace high above,
O'erwhelm Thy suppliants in
flames:
Our hearts devour by Thy love
And with love's martyrs count our
names.

Amor, Pater clementiæ,
Amor, Redemptor omnium,
Amor, Deus, fons gratiæ,
Regnes in omne sæculum.
                          Amen.

O Love, of mercy sweet the Sire,
O Love, Redeemer of all men;
O Love, of God the grace and fire,
Forever and forever reign!
                          Amen.

V. Omnis spiritus laudet Cor
Jesu et Mariæ.
R. Et diligant illud omnia corda.

V. Let every soul praise the
Hearts of Jesus and Mary.
R. And every heart love them.

Ad. Magnif. Ant. Tibi laus, tibi honor, tibi gloria, o amantissime Jesu, qui dedisti Cor tuum dilectissimæ Matri tuæ; ut ipsa tibi uno Corde in salutem humanam cooperans, digna Salvatoris Mater effici mereretur, alleluia.

Ant. Praise, honor and glory to Thee, O beloved Jesus, Who didst give Thy Heart to Thy beloved Mother, that she, being one in heart with Thee and cooperating in the salvation of the human race, might merit to become the worthy Mother of the Saviour of the world, alleluia.

Oratio: Pater misericordiarum et Deus totius consolationis. . . .

Oration: Father of Mercies and God of all consolation. . . .

PRAYERS

TO

THE SACRED HEART OF JESUS

LITANY OF THE SACRED HEART OF JESUS

Kyrie, eleison.

Lord, have mercy on us.

Christe, eleison.

Christ, have mercy on us.

Kyrie, eleison.

Lord, have mercy on us.

Jesu, audi nos.

Jesus, hear us.

Jesu, exaudi nos.

Jesus, graciously hear us.

Pater, de cælis Deus, miserere nobis.

God, the Father of heaven, have mercy on us.

Fili, Redemptor mundi, Deus, miserere nobis.

God the Son, Redeemer of the world, have mercy on us.

Spiritus Sancte Deus, miserere nobis.

God the Holy Ghost, have mercy on us.

Sancta Trinitas, unus Deus, miserere nobis.

Holy Trinity, one God, have mercy on us.

Cor Jesu divinissimum, miserere nobis.

Heart of Jesus most divine, have mercy on us.

Cor Jesu amantissimum.

Heart of Jesus most loving,

Cor Jesu mitissimum,

Heart of Jesus most meek,

Cor Jesus humillimum,

Heart of Jesus, most humble,

Cor Jesu misericordissimum,

Heart of Jesus most merciful,

Cor Jesu fidelissimum,

Heart of Jesus most faithful,

Cor Jesu, cor Patris æterni,

Heart of Jesus, Heart of the Eternal Father,

Cor Jesu, origo Spiritus sancti,

Heart of Jesus, Principle of the Holy Ghost,

Cor Jesu, plenitudo Divinitatis,

Heart of Jesus, fullness of the Godhead,

Cor Jesu, sanctuarium Trinitatis,	Heart of Jesus, sanctuary of the Blessed Trinity,
Cor Jesu, thronus divinæ Voluntatis,	Heart of Jesus, throne of the Divine Will,
Cor Jesu, Cor Virginis Matris	Heart of Jesus, Heart of the Virgin Mother,
Cor Jesu adorabile,	Heart of Jesus most adorable,
Cor Jesu amabile,	Heart of Jesus most amiable,
Cor Jesu admirabile,	Heart of Jesus most admirable,
Cor Jesu incomparabile,	Heart of Jesus most incomparable,
Cor Jesu, fornax amoris,	Heart of Jesus, furnace of love,
Cor Jesu, miraculum caritatis,	Heart of Jesus, miracle of charity,
Cor Jesu, norma patientiæ,	Heart of Jesus, model of patience,
Cor Jesu, speculum obedientiæ,	Heart of Jesus, mirror of obedience,
Cor Jesu, exemplar virtutum,	Heart of Jesus, exemplar of all virtues,
Cor Jesu, fons omnium gratiarum,	Heart of Jesus, fountain of all graces,
Cor Jesu, lancea transfixum,	Heart of Jesus, pierced with a lance,
Cor Jesu, amore vulneratum,	Heart of Jesus, wounded with love,
Cor Jesu, templum sanctitatis,	Heart of Jesus, temple of sanctity,
Cor Jesu, altare caritatis,	Heart of Jesus, altar of charity,
Cor Jesu, sacerdos amoris,	Heart of Jesus, priest of love,
Cor Jesu, hostia dilectionis,	Heart of Jesus, victim of dilection,
Cor Jesu, holocaustum æternum,	Heart of Jesus, eternal holocaust,
Cor Jesu, thuribulum aureum,	Heart of Jesus, golden censer,
Cor Jesu, calix inebrians,	Heart of Jesus, inebriating chalice,
Cor Jesu, nectar deificans,	Heart of Jesus, deifying nectar,

Cor Jesu, consolator afflictorum,	Heart of Jesus, consoler of the afflicted,
Cor Jesu, refugium peccatorum,	Heart of Jesus, refuge of sinners,
Cor Jesu, zelator animarum,	Heart of Jesus, zealous for souls,
Cor Jesu, raptor cordium,	Heart of Jesus, ravisher of hearts,
Cor Jesu, pars nostra carissima,	Heart of Jesus, our dearest portion,
Cor Jesu, spes nostra dulcissima,	Heart of Jesus, our sweetest hope,
Cor Jesu, cordis nostri gaudium,	Heart of Jesus, joy of our heart,
Cor Jesu, cordis nostri Cor dilectissimum,	Heart of Jesus, most loving Heart of our heart,
Cor Jesu, cordis nostri thesaurus,	Heart of Jesus, treasure of our heart,
Cor Jesu, cordis nostri paradisus,	Heart of Jesus, paradise of our heart,
Cor Jesu, vita cordis nostri,	Heart of Jesus, life of our heart,
Cor Jesu, rex cordis nostri,	Heart of Jesus, king of our heart,
Propitius esto, parce· nobis, Jesu.	Be merciful unto us, spare us, O Jesus.
Propitius esto, exaudi nos, Jesu.	Be merciful unto us, graciously hear us, O Jesus.
Ab omni peccato, libera nos, Jesu.	From all sin, deliver us, O Jesus.
A superbia vitæ, libera nos, Jesu.	From the pride of life, deliver us, O Jesus.
Ab inordinato amore,	From disordinate love,
A cæcitate cordis,	From the blindness of heart,
A neglectu inspirationum tuarum,	From the neglect of Thy inspirations,
A morte perpetua,	From everlasting death,
Per Cor tuum amantissimum, exaudi nos, Jesu.	Through Thy most loving Heart, hear us, O Jesus.
Per maximum ejus in peccatum odium,	Through Thy great hatred for sin, hear us, O Jesus.

Per infinitum ejus in Patrem æternum amorem,

Through Thy infinite love for Thy Eternal Father,

Per dulcissimam ejus in sanctissimam Matrem dilectionem,

Through Thy tender love for Thy most holy Mother,

Per ardentissimam illius erga sibi devotos charitatem, exaudi nos Jesu.

Through thy most ardent charity for all those who are devoted to Thy service, hear us, O Jesus.

Per summum ejus erga crucem affectum,

Through Thy great love for the Cross.

Per acerbissimos dolores ipsius,

Through Thy bitter sufferings,

Per ipsum amoris et doloris impetu pro nobis in morte disruptum,

Through Thy death out of love and sorrow for us,

Per æterna ejus gaudia,

Through Thy eternal joys,

Agnus Dei, qui tollis peccata mundi, parce nobis, Jesu.

Lamb of God, who takest away the sins of the world, spare us, O Jesus.

Agnus Dei, qui tollis peccata mundi, exaudi nos, Jesu.

Lamb of God, who takest away the sins of the world, graciously hear us, O Jesus.

Agnus Dei, qui tollis peccata mundi, miserere nobis, Jesu.

Lamb of God, who takest away the sins of the world, have mercy on us, O Jesus.

Jesu, audi nos.
Jesu, exaudi nos.

Jesus, hear us.
Jesus, graciously hear us.

Oremus

Deus, qui propter nimiam caritatem tuam nos Unigeniti tui membra et filios tuos efficiens, Cor unum cum Capite et Patre nostro habere voluisti: præsta, quæsumus, ut igne tui amoris et flamma caritatis Cordis amantissimi Jesu accensi tuam in omnibus Voluntatem corde magno adimpleamus, et quæ recta sunt desiderantes, desiderata percipere mereamur. Per eumdem Christum Dominum nostrum.
Amen.

Let us pray

O God, who by the great love of Thy only-begotten Son hast willed to make us Thy members and Thy sons and hast given us one Heart with Thy Head and our Father, grant, we beseech Thee, that burning with the fire of Thy love and the flame of the charity of the most loving Heart of Jesus we may do Thy will in all things, and desiring what is right we may merit to obtain what we desire. Through the same Christ Our Lord. Amen.

SALUTATION TO THE SACRED HEARTS OF JESUS AND MARY

"This salutation is a beautiful consecration to the Sacred Heart of Jesus and to the Holy Heart of Mary. Although the Heart of the Son is infinitely superior in excellence and sanctity to the Heart of the Mother, God has united these two Hearts so closely that they are always one single Heart in feeling, affection and will. Moreover, Jesus lives and reigns so completely in the Heart of Mary that He is truly the soul of her soul, the spirit of her spirit, and the heart of her heart. Thus, we may rightly say that Jesus is the Heart of Mary and salute and revere Jesus in her as the spirit, the soul, the life, and the Heart of His Holy Mother." Cf. *Oeuvres Complètes*, VIII, pp. 363-364.

"Furthermore, when in this salutation I use the words, *Adoramus te,* the reader must not be surprised. There are three kinds of adoration or worship: the worship of *latria,* which is paid exclusively to God; *hyperdulia,* which is the special reverence with which we honor the Blessed Virgin Mary; and *dulia,* which is the respect paid to the saints. Do not think that when you say the words, *Adoramus te,* we are paying the same reverence and respect to the Sacred Heart of Jesus and to the Holy Heart of Mary. To the Sacred Heart we owe the supreme worship that is paid exclusively to God because of His uncreated and infinite excellence; to the Holy Heart of Mary we pay special worship, on account of her created but pre-eminent excellence." Cf. *Oeuvres Complètes*, VIII, pp. 491-492.

Ave, Cor sanctissimum,	Hail, Heart most holy,
Ave, Cor mitissimum,	Hail, Heart most meek,
Ave, Cor humillimum,	Hail, Heart most humble,
Ave, Cor purissimum,	Hail, Heart most pure,
Ave, Cor devotissimum,	Hail, Heart most devout,
Ave, Cor sapientissimum,	Hail, Heart most wise,
Ave, Cor patientissimum,	Hail, Heart most patient,
Ave, Cor obedientissimum,	Hail, Heart most obedient,
Ave, Cor vigilantissimum,	Hail, Heart most vigilant,
Ave, Cor fidelissimum,	Hail, Heart most faithful,
Ave, Cor beatissimum,	Hail, Heart most blessed,
Ave, Cor misericordissimum,	Hail, Heart most merciful,
Ave, Cor amantissimum Jesu et Mariæ;	Hail, most loving Heart of Jesus and Mary;
Te adoramus,	We revere Thee,
Te laudamus,	We praise Thee,
Te glorificamus,	We glorify Thee,
Tibi gratias agimus;	We give Thee thanks;

Te amamus,
Ex toto corde nostro,
Ex tota anima nostra,
Et ex totis viribus nostris;
Tibi cor nostrum offerimus,
Donamus,
Consecramus,
Immolamus;
Accipe et posside illud totum,
Et purifica,
Et illumina,
Et sanctifica;
    Ut in ipso vivas et regnes et nunc
et semper, et in sæcula sæculorum.
Amen.

We love Thee,
With all our heart,
With all our soul,
And with all our strength;
We offer Thee our heart,
We give it to Thee,
We consecrate it to Thee,
We immolate it to Thee;
Receive it and possess it wholly,
Purify it,
Enlighten it,
Sanctify it;
    That Thou mayest live and reign
in it now, always, and forever and
ever. Amen.

MAGNIFICAT OF SAINT JOHN EUDES

A Hymn of Praise and Thanksgiving to the Sacred Heart of Jesus and to the Holy Heart of Mary

Magnificat anima mea Cor admirabile Jesu et Mariæ,

My soul doth magnify the admirable Heart of Jesus and Mary,

Et exsultavit spiritus meus in magno Corde meo.

And my spirit rejoices in my great Heart.

Nam Cor suum maximum dederunt mihi Jesus et Maria, ut omnia mea, in caritate ejus fiant.

Jesus and Mary have given me their Heart, this immense Heart in order that all in me may be performed in its love.

Gratias illis infinitas super inenarrabili dono ipsorum.

Infinite thanks to them for their ineffable gift.

Fecit mihi magna Cor benignissimum; suscepit me ab utero matris meæ.

This Heart infinitely merciful has done great things for me; it has possessed me from the womb of my mother.

Gratias infinitas super inenerrabilibus donis ejus.

Infinite thanks for His ineffable gifts.

Abyssus miseriarum mearum invocavit abyssum misericordiarum ejus.

The abyss of my misery has called on the abyss of His mercy.

Gratias infinitas super inenarrabilibus donis ejus.

Infinite thanks for His ineffable gifts.

Prævenit me Cor mitissimum in benedictionibus dulcedinis suæ.

This Heart infinitely meek has presented me with blessings of its sweetness.

Gratias infinitas super inenarrabilibus donis ejus.

Infinite thanks for His ineffable gifts.

Sub umbra manus suæ protexit me, et custodivit me quasi pupillam oculi.

He has protected me in the shadow of His Hand, and has guarded me as the apple of His eye.

Gratias infinitas super inenarrabilibus donis ejus.

Infinite thanks for His ineffable gifts.

Elegit me sacerdotem sibi et cum principibus sui collocavit me.

He has chosen me to be His priest and has placed me with the princes of His people.

Gratias infinitas super inenarrabilibus donis ejus.

Infinite thanks for His ineffable gifts.

Dedit verba sua in ore meo et posuit os meum quasi gladium acutum.

He has placed His words in my mouth and my tongue was like unto a sharp sword.

Gratias infinitas super inenarrabilibus donis ejus.

Infinite thanks for His ineffable gifts.

Mortificavit et vivificavit me et fuit mecum ubicumque ambulavi.

He has led me to the valley of death and recalled me to life and He has been with me wherever I have directed my steps.

Gratias infinitas super inenarrabilibus donis ejus.

Infinite thanks for His ineffable gifts.

Inimicus fuit inimicis meis et ex omnibus tribulationibus meis liberavit me.

He has been the enemy of my enemies and has delivered me from all my tribulations.

Gratias infinitas super inenarrabilibus donis ejus.

Infinite thanks for his ineffable gifts.

O Cor amantissimum, fons omnium bonorum, a te mihi venerunt innumera bona.

O loving Heart, source of all good, it is from Thee that all good has come to me.

Tibi laus, tibi amor, tibi gloria, te omnes linguæ concinant, te diligant omnia corda.

Praise, love and glory to Thee, and may all tongues sing Thy benefits and may all hearts burn with Thy love.

Confiteantur tibi misericordiæ tuæ: et amoris tui mirabilia filiis hominum.

May Thy mercies be praised and may the marvels of Thy love be distributed among the children of men.

Benedicant te omnes virtutes tuæ: laudent et superexaltant in sæcula.

May all Thy virtues bless Thee and praise and exalt Thee above all forever.

Memor sit Pater misericordiarum omnis sacrificii tui: et tribuat tibi cuncta desideria tua.

May the Father of Mercies remember all Thy sacrifices and grant all Thy desires.

O Cor Jesu, amoris et doloris impetu pro nobis in cruce disruptum: tibi cor nostrum in igne tuo perpetuo immoletur.

O Heart of Jesus broken for us upon the Cross by the violence of Thy love and suffering, may our hearts consumed by Thy love be a perpetual holocaust.

O Cor Mariæ, doloris gladio transfixum! fac ut cor nostrum divini amoris sagitta jugiter transfigatur.

O Heart of Mary pierced with a sword of sorrow, may our hearts be continually pierced with the arrow of divine love.

O Cor Jesu et Mariæ, fornax amoris! in te cor nostrum demergatur in perpetuum.

O Heart of Jesus and Mary, furnace of love, may our heart be forever plunged in your fires.

Moriatur in flammis tuis, ut cum Corde Jesu et Mariæ cor unum fiat in æternum.

May it die in your flames that it may be one with the Heart of Jesus and Mary for all eternity.

Gloria Patri et Filio et Spiritui Sancto.

Glory be to the Father and to the Son and to the Holy Ghost.

Sicut erat in principio et nunc et semper et in sæcula sæculorum. Amen.

As it was in the beginning, is now, and ever shall be world without end. Amen.

ORATIO POST OFFICIUM

O clementissime Jesu, gratias ago tibi ex toto corde meo. Propitius esto mihi vilissimo peccatori. Ego hanc actionem offero divino Cordi tuo emandandam atque perficiendam, ad laudem et gloriam sanctissimi Nominis tui et beatissimæ Matris tuæ, ad salutem animæ meæ totiusque Ecclesiæ tuæ. Amen.

PRAYER AFTER THE DIVINE OFFICE

O most clement Jesus, I thank Thee with my whole heart for all Thy graces. Be propitious unto me a sinner. I offer this action to Thy Sacred Heart to be emended and perfected, for the praise and glory of Thy Holy Name and of that of Thy Blessed Mother, for the salvation of my soul, and for the whole church. Amen.

INVOCATIO

Benedictum sit Cor amantissimum et dulcissimum Nomen Domini nostri Jesu Christi, et glorissimæ Virginis Mariæ ejus, in æternum et ultra.

EJACULATORY PRAYER

Blessed be forever the most loving Hearts and the sweet Names of our Lord Jesus Christ and of the most glorious Virgin Mary, His Mother.

APPENDIX

Excerpts from Papal Documents concerning St. John Eudes and the Devotion to the Sacred Heart of Jesus:

Auctor cultus liturgici sacrorum Cordium. "The institutor of the liturgical worship of the Sacred Hearts."—Leo XIII in the *Decree on the Heroism of the Virtues of John Eudes,* January 6, 1903.

"But his services to the Church received a vast increase when, burning with a singular love for the most holy Hearts of Jesus and Mary, *he was the first to think, not without some divine inspiration, of offering to them liturgical worship. Of this sweet devotion of piety,* therefore, *he is to be considered the father,* since from the beginning of his congregation of priests he provided that the feasts of those Sacred Hearts should be celebrated among them; *the doctor* also, for he composed special offices and masses in their honor; and finally *the apostle,* for he strove with all his might to spread everywhere this salutary devotion."—Pius X in the *Decree of Beatification,* December 13, 1908.

"His zeal was manifested in a singular manner in promoting the salutary devotion to the Sacred Hearts of Jesus and Mary. He was the *first to think,* not without some divine inspiration, *of rendering them liturgical worship.* . . . The zeal of John Eudes reached its peak when in *1670, after a mission at Rennes* and the foundation of a seminary in that town, *he was able there to celebrate for the first time the Feast of the Sacred Heart of Jesus,* with the approval of the Ordinary, with which a great number of prelates hastened to concur. Two years later, the saintly founder explicitly ordained that the Feast be celebrated in all the houses of his congregation as the patronal feast. Pius X, Our Predecessor of illustrious memory, sanctioned these two feasts, celebrated by the Eudistic family, and authorized as the day of the solemnity, February 8 for the Feast of the Holy Heart of Mary, and October 20 for the Sacred Heart of Jesus. This endeavour to spread the devotion to the Sacred Hearts, of which *he is the Father, the Doctor and the Apostle,* stirred up the hatred of the Jansenists, who made him suffer many trials; his invincible courage supported them for the love of God and the salvation of souls."— Pius XI in the *Decree of Canonization,* May 31, 1925.

"Lastly, in more recent centuries, especially at the time when heretics by propagating false piety were striving to turn the faithful away from the Blessed Eucharist, the public devotion to the Sacred Heart saw its beginnings. This was due primarily to the work of St. John Eudes, who rightly deserves to be called the institutor of the liturgical worship of the Sacred Hearts of Jesus and Mary."—*Office for the Feast of the Sacred Heart of Jesus,* Matins, Second Nocturn, Lesson 4.

INDEX

THE GREAT COMMENTARY
on THE FOUR GOSPELS
by Cornelius aLapide, S.J.

QUOTES FROM THE REVIEW by SCOTT HAHN

Cornelius aLapide, S.J. (1568-1637) is a giant figure in the history of Catholic biblical interpretation. Born in a tiny Catholic enclave in the Calvinist Netherlands in the bloody generation after the Reformation, Lapide grew to be one of the Church's most gifted scholars and spiritual interpreters of the sacred page.

Between 1614 and 1645, Lapide wrote commentaries on every book of Scripture except Job and Psalms.

To read Lapide four hundred years later is to enter a nearly forgotten world of biblical interpretation ...more striking – the sheer breadth and density of Lapide's interpretative matrix or his audacity in summoning all these resources to the interpretation of the sacred text.

Lapide himself takes a breathtaking high view of Scripture's purpose: Lapide prefaces his commentary with thirty-eight "canons of interpretation," which reflect a wise and prayerful method. "

It is clear that the Fathers hold pride of place for Lapide in his interpretative work.

- *6"x 9" Book format*
- *2900+ Pages in four volumes*
- *First complete English translation*
- *Sewn Binding & Headbands*
- *Bonded Leather Covers &*
    Satin Ribbons
- *Greatest Catholic Bible*
    Commentary ever
- *Extensive discussion of Greek and Hebrew words*
- *$199. Per four volume set*